Finding the Balance in World Missions

↭

Written By
Steven E. Ray, Director-Pastor

A Publication of
Messiah Missions International

Finding the Balance in World Missions

Copyright © 2012 by Steven E. Ray. The Messiah Missions logo is a registered trademark of Messiah Missions International, Inc.

All rights reserved. No part of this book may be reproduced in any form or by any electronic or mechanical means, including information storage and retrieval systems, without written permission from the publisher or author, except in the case of a reviewer, who may quote brief passages embodied in critical articles or in a review. Author may be contacted through www.messiahmissions.org.

Some of the anecdotal illustrations in this book are true to life and are included with the permission of the person or persons involved. All other illustrations are composites of real situations, and any resemblance of people living or dead is purely coincidental.

Scripture quotations are from The Holy Bible, English Standard Version® (ESV®) unless otherwise noted, copyright © 2001 by Crossway, a publishing ministry of Good News Publishers. Used by permission. All rights reserved.

Cover design using Adobe Photoshop CS6 and interior pagination using Adobe InDesign CS6 by author Steven E. Ray

Publisher on record at Bowker Link:
Primedia E-Launch
3900 Swiss Ave #205, Dallas, Texas 75204
A publication of Messiah Missions International.

First Edition Booklet 2012
Second Edition Book 2013
Third Edition Unabridged 2014

ISBN-10 1-622-09205-8
ISBN-13 978-1-62209-205-5

Translated from English into Kannada and Spanish as of 2014. Others forthcoming.
Printed in the United States of America.

Table of Contents

Foreword 5
Author's Preface 7
1] Evangelism Defined 11
2] Traditional Evangelism Methods 17
3] Postmodern Evangelism Methods 23
4] Asking Questions in Evangelism 29
5] Open-Air Evangelism 35
6] Spirituality around the World 43
7] The Challenge of Syncretism 51
8] Evangelism and Philanthropy 59
9] The Problem of the Social Gospel 67
10] The Enemy verses the Power of God 75
11] Good Intentions without Discernment 81
12] Persuaded to Share Christ 87
13] A Call to Repentance 95
14] The Scriptures and Evangelism 101
15] The Holy Spirit in Evangelism 111
16] Prayer Essential for Evangelism 119
17] Direction under God's Spirit 127
18] Suffering and Persecutions 135
19] Scriptural Benevolence in Missions 143
20] The Indigenous Church 151
21] Support of the Indigenous Leadership 159
22] Field Mission's Leadership Qualifications 169
23] How May I Get Involved? 175

Foreword

Jesus, our beloved Lord, taught a message of repentance and provided the remission of sins, telling His disciples to proclaim the good news to the entire world. The power of God through Christ can regenerate an individual, restore a family, reform a society and transform a nation.

When Jesus commanded His disciples to go and preach, they did not take it as a white collar job. They did not seek out summer resorts or recreational suburbs, nor did they start building schools and hospitals. They understood the importance of the message and had to obey the Lord who told them, "*I will build my Church.*" They were co-workers in the building work of the eternal and living mansions.

The beginning of the 20th century witnessed latter rains of the Holy Ghost revival and many converts went out as missionaries. But where are all the great masses of confessing converts today? Where is the whole fruit of evangelization? Are all the Nations of the world evangelized having heard the good news? What to do and how? This spiritual rich book strives to examine these questions and arrive at conclusions.

Finding the Balance in World Missions deals with highly relevant contemporary missions' issues we are faced within the Church. Although small in size, its content addresses many of the problems facing the modern Church. World missions should not target only third world countries, the 10-40 Window, or the Far East alone. In the last 20 years the Church of England has lost nearly three in every ten of its members. These same statistics are echoed in the Church of Scotland. By contrast the Roman Catholics in England, the Methodists and the United Reformed have all lost nearly four in every ten. Missionaries are now needed in the very areas from where they were once sent from.

We are grateful for the missionaries who did not lose their God ordained vision. If David Livingston had sought comfort, another hospital could have been erected in India or Cambodia, and Africa would have remained a spiritually dark continent. If William Carey loved only his life, he could have fulfilled his dreams and settled down in Serampore located in West Bengal. However, due to his dedication to soul winning, widows in North India were delivered from being roasted in flames on a funeral pyre. A practice called Sati, where a widowed woman would immolate herself on her husband's funeral pyre. Additionally, William convinced Lord Wellesley to outlaw the practice of casting live babies to the alligators into the Ganges River as a human sacrifice.

Finding the Balance in World Missions is an immensely readable and challenging work about evangelism and missions. Rev. Ray's intelligent, well researched and informed approach ensures that the search for understanding the biblical approach to missions fully engages our minds as well as our hearts.

I am honored in commending this practical field manual to the pastors, teachers and evangelists to read prayerfully, study carefully and follow the Lord's guidance with tears of humility, as we toil together in fulfilling the Great Commission. This book will help guide the mission-minded on the right course, finding the direction God has for their life, helping yield the fruits the Lord promised. *"Well done, you faithful servant: because you were found faithful"* (Luke 19:17).

Pastor John Madan Mohan
Nanjangud, India

Author's Preface

Finding the Balance in World Missions was developed over time as a divinely inspired book (prayerfully intended) that purposes to convey God's revelation about the biblical model of missions and evangelism as presented in Scripture. As a field manual or instructional text, this book was written for the purpose of training missionaries and indigenous pastors about the important details of international missions.

The chapters are segmented into carefully organized and sequential parts, laden with author quotes and annotated with scriptural references. The material first examines the modern, then historical methods of evangelism, which is an important component of biblical missions. Chapter six begins looking at the current condition of world spirituality and the Church, moving into chapter eleven which focuses more on the Christian's personal involvement within missions. The last few chapters examine the structure and missional obligations of the global Church unto the indigenous church, the missionary, the native pastor and the purpose of supporting organizations.

Modern missions including the role of evangelism is far more challenging than we might initially perceive. Most missiologies (studies of missions) have been written from a mono-cultural perspective where the West (referencing Europe, North America and Oceania) was assumed to be center stage. This is primarily due to the lack of global perspective, something this book seeks to remedy—adjusting views that lack international exposure. Because of the rise of postmodernism in the Church, ongoing redefinitions modify the purpose of missions, requiring us to carefully examine the revised methods against biblical revelation.

There are multiple trends that have affected missions, originating namely from the West, which have resulted in some confusion and gradual departure from sound missiology. Initially, there is a general malaise and regression of traditional Christianity in what used to be sending nations. Additionally, the West has been slow to grasp the full missiological implications of the simultaneous emergence of the post-Christian and post-western Christianity.

According to Ed Vitagliano, news editor for *American Family Association Journal*, he noted in 2004 how Christianity is waning in the West because of the "advancing assault of secularism and New Age spirituality." However, at the same time, he explained of a developing phenomenon: that Christianity is growing in the part of the world called 'Global South' – Africa, Latin America and Asia – and in the next 50 years he surmised those regions would become the new "spiritual frontier of faith." For example, in the year 1900, there were approximately 10 million Christians on the African continent, but by 2000, the number had grown to 360 million. In terms of evangelical Christians, who are recognized as the most thriving group within the Christian community, he noted that 70% of them live outside of the Western sphere of influence.

As the biblical traditions which shaped the Church break down, one of the predominant advances in missions is the humanitarian social manifesto, a mindset that has replaced biblical evangelism with the revived 'Social Gospel' movement. This notably results in churches that focus more on social works instead of first being grounded in biblical discipleship, leading with evangelism as the main purpose. What has spawned in the wake of the progressive church is the simultaneous deconstruction of denominational identities along with the emergence of a multiplicity of autonomous bodies that redefine traditional biblical standards. These changes result in a definitive challenge for missions.

The purpose of this book is to help the reader realize that the work of missions is primarily God's Triune work to guide and empower, not ours. Evangelism and missions are God's

[Author's Preface]

redemptive, historical initiative on behalf of His creation. *Missio Dei,* is a popular Latin Christian theological term used among missiologists, is thus pertinent, which can be translated as the 'mission of God,' or the 'sending of God.' Missiology must be articulated from a theological and theocentric framework found in Scripture. The social sciences and articulated business models can be helpful, but the Bible will always be the guidebook, the final revelation of God's divine purposes.

The Father of Creation is the sender as Lord of the harvest; the incarnate Son Jesus Christ is the whole embodiment of a missionary-evangelist going into the world; and the Holy Spirit is the divine, empowering presence for all of mission's work. Anything more or anything less can quickly result in a departure from the biblical revelation given once unto the Saints regarding the Great Commission.

Prayerfully, the insights and discussions from this book will inspire, convict, and awaken slumbering souls to devote themselves to God according to His manifested will. There are many genuine followers of Jesus who desire to understand with spiritual clarity about how to approach evangelism and missions as Jesus would have us. May the Lord guide you to find His will within the divine calling over your life.

[FINDING THE BALANCE IN WORLD MISSIONS]

[1]
EVANGELISM DEFINED

In order to understand missions, we must first have a proper understanding of evangelism. Please be careful to consider the first few chapters of this book which look deeply into the essential details of evangelism before moving into the subject of global missions.

We understand that the single purpose of the Church is to glorify God and one of the active ways to glorify God, according to the Bible, is through evangelism. African missionary David Livingston aptly stated, "God had only one Son and He made that Son a missionary." God the Father is an evangelist at heart as Christ Jesus reflected by the Spirit, when reading Isaiah 61:1-2, *"The Spirit of the Lord GOD is upon me, because the LORD has anointed me to bring good news to the poor; he has sent me to bind up the brokenhearted, to proclaim liberty to the captives, and the opening of the prison to those who are bound; to proclaim the year of the LORD's favor, and the day of vengeance of our God; to comfort all who mourn."*

Evangelism is synonymous with missions, the overriding term that encompasses local evangelism, regional evangelism, and international evangelism. While evangelism is usually regarded as converting non-Christians to Christianity, this is not the only usage of the word. Islam, Buddhism and other faiths are evangelistic by nature, but the term is most often used in reference to Christianity.

To understand the word 'evangelism' we have to look at the word 'gospel.' The word *gospel* derives from the Old English *gōd-spell*, meaning 'good news' or 'glad tidings.' It is a word-for-word translation of the Greek word *euangelion* (eu- 'good', -angelion 'message'), which is the source of the terms 'evangelist' and 'evangelism' in English. The authors of the four canonical Christian Gospels are also known as the four evangelists who spoke a message of 'good news.'

One of the challenges in defining the words *mission* or *missionary* according to a biblical context is that they are not found in the Bible. The root word comes from a Latin verb, '*mitto*,' meaning 'to send.' It is the equivalent of the Greek word *apostle*, which also means 'to send.' The root word of the two words is identical. The word apostle occurs more than eighty times in the New Testament. In one place it refers to Christ (Hebrews 3:1). Jesus Christ was the first Apostle, deriving His apostleship from the Father who, He said on many occasions, 'sent' Him into the world on a mission of redemption.

Evangelist in the modern Church is often a title for one that travels from town to town and from church to church, spreading the gospel of Jesus Christ. Many Christians of various theological perspectives would call themselves evangelists because they are active in sharing the gospel. The title of evangelist has historically been associated with those who lead large meetings like the Billy Graham Crusades or, as of recent years, Greg Laurie and his simulcast Harvest Crusades. Evangelists may meet in tents, existing church buildings, or are those individuals who address the public while conducting street corner preaching. Evangelism can also be initiated within small groups or even on a one-to-one basis, but fundamentally the meaning of the word represents one that spreads the gospel.

Contrary to popular belief, Evangelists are not only servants who are specially gifted and called by God to provide all the evangelizing for the Church of Jesus Christ. Evangelists are those who equip the saints for the work of service. They are those who teach the Body of Christ, the Church, how to evangelize biblically. Paul wrote in Eph. 4:11-12, *"And He gave some as apostles, and some as prophets, and some as evangelists, and some as pastors and teachers, for*

[EVANGELISM DEFINED]

the equipping of the saints for the work of service, to the building up of the body of Christ."

Overall, Christian evangelism is the proclamation of the substitutionary sacrifice of Jesus' life for our sins, in such a way that people receive, repent and commit their lives to Jesus Christ as Lord (master of life) and Savior (redeemer of souls); submitting to the public act of baptism and then becoming united with a biblically-sound body of believers.

From the New Testament, we gain a sense that once a person had become a Christian, it was a natural persuasion for them to speak of their faith with others. There were no required schools of learning before they began sharing their faith, only a genuine encounter and conversion through the Spirit of the Lord Jesus Christ. While ongoing biblical training with seasoned Christians is always necessary through discipleship, it is God's prerogative that we share the gospel as moved by the indwelling Holy Spirit at any time.

Devote Christians consider it their obligation to obey what is often termed the 'Great Commission' declared by Jesus, recorded in the final verses of the Gospel of Matt. 28:19-20: *"Go therefore and make disciples of all nations, baptizing them in the name of the Father and of the Son and of the Holy Spirit, teaching them to observe all that I have commanded you. And behold, I am with you always, to the end of the age."* The New Testament urges believers to speak the gospel clearly, fearlessly, graciously, and respectfully whenever an opportunity presents itself (see Col. 4:2–6, Eph. 6:19–20, and I Peter 3:15).

The Acts of the Apostles and other sources contain several accounts of early Christians following this directive by engaging in individual conversations and large open-air sermons to spread the good news. Evangelical Christians often use the term 'witnessing' or 'to give a firsthand account of something seen, heard, or experienced' which evangelistically means discussing one's faith with another person with the intent of engaging a soul for God's glory.

[FINDING THE BALANCE IN WORLD MISSIONS]

The Barna Group, who is an evangelical visionary research and resource company based in Ventura, CA, has charted evangelistic practices and attitudes of Christians since 1984. When asked if they have a personal responsibility to share their faith with others, 73% of born again Christians said yes. When this conviction is put into practice, however, the numbers shift downward. Only half (52%) of born again Christians say they actually did share the Gospel at least once this past year to someone with different beliefs, in the hope that they might accept Jesus Christ as their Savior. As with most convictions, there usually lies a divide between theory and practice.

David J. Bosch in his 1991 book *Transforming Mission* wrote, "Missions is not primarily an activity of the Church, but an attribute of God. God is a missionary God." During the past half century, there has been a subtle but nevertheless decisive shift away from understanding missions as God's mission. During preceding centuries, missions was defined in a variety of ways. Sometimes it was interpreted primarily in soteriological terms as saving souls from eternal damnation. Often it was perceived in ecclesiastical categories as the expansion of the Church. In all these varied instances and frequently conflicting ways, the intrinsic interrelationship between Christology, soteriology, and the doctrine of the Trinity was gradually displaced by various redefinitions.

Missions and evangelism should be understood as being derived from the very nature of God. The classical doctrine on the *Missio Dei* as God the Father sending the Son, and God the Father and the Son sending the Spirit was expanded to include the Father, Son and the Holy Spirit sending the Church into the world. Mission is thereby seen as a movement from God to the world; the Church is viewed as an instrument for that mission. There is Church because there is mission, not vice versa. To participate in mission is to participate in the movement of God's love toward his beloved children.

[EVANGELISM DEFINED]

Throughout most of Christianity's history, the faith has grown evangelistically, though the extent of evangelism has varied significantly among Christian communities and denominations. Sadly, even though many understand the tenants of evangelism fairly well, there is an unuttered myth in missions. Jesus told us that the field is the world (Matt. 13:38), but the Church often divides the field into two parts, home and foreign. In general context, a missionary is considered a person who is called to share the gospel in a foreign country. Those who would serve local street people must settle for a less exotic appellation. Keith R. Bridgton wrote in his book **Mission Myth and Reality**, "The mission of the Church was so closely identified with geographical expansion, and the missionary enterprise so exclusively considered in terms of the geographical frontiers, that the term "missions" inevitably had a foreign connotation."

Over time, the local Church has at times surrounded foreign missions with an aura of sacredness not readily shared with any other forms of Christian outreach. Any missionary serving in the 10/40 zone (the term refers to those regions of the eastern hemisphere, and the European and African part of the western hemisphere, located between 10 and 40 degrees north of the equator) may carry an appeal as a "genuine missionary" over those of other locations. This is unfortunate, for it polarizes the missionary enterprise into two separate entities, one superior to the other.

Another problem glossed over is due to humanistic influences reshaping the Church with certain aspects of postmodernism. The modern consumeristic Church often places more emphasis on self-edification, personal success and looking after one's own physical needs and pleasures versus proclaiming the good news of Jesus Christ as personal Savior. Additionally, the Church Growth Movement continues to give more attention to social relevance, which encourages its adherents to refrain from any "fanatical offense" as it has been referred. The biblical pattern for the sanctified growth of Christ's body (the Church) is sometimes ignored, substituted with social sciences, business strategies and marketing techniques. Modern institutions (the Church) are regularly being converted into morally framed social clubs under the guise of "religious tolerance" as the message about salvation, eternal hell and sin as presented in Scripture is pruned away as offensive.

As a result of misguided leadership which leads to a grave departure from biblical Christianity, consumeristic evangelism yields scores of false Christians. Pastor Dennis James Kennedy of Coral Ridge Presbyterian Church in Fort Lauderdale, Florida, said before his passing:

> The vast majority of people who are members of churches in America today are not Christians. I say that without the slightest contradiction. I base it on empirical evidence of twenty-four years of examining thousands of people.

Evangelism is the hope of the Church, hence the hope of the world. The vital importance of New Testament evangelism is emphasized by the testimony of the centuries, namely the Church which ceases to be biblically evangelistic will soon cease to be evangelical and thus biblical.

[2]
TRADITIONAL EVANGELISM METHODS

Christianity is sometimes described as a "Western religion," meaning that it has been influential primarily in the West in reference of Europe, North America and Oceania. Indeed, at the beginning of this century, 64% of all Christians lived in Europe and North America. Even today Asian Christians now make up only 10% of global Christians. In their own countries Asian Christians represent a mere 3.5% of the population of Asia. Therefore in most of Asia, Christianity is a minority religion scattered throughout other cultures.

We are going to take some time to review traditional Western Christian evangelism methods, since they are often the catalyst for methods used globally. They include the **Romans Road**, Dr. James Kennedy's *Evangelism Explosion*, Campus Crusade and their *Four Spiritual Laws*, and the Navigators method called *The Bridge to Life*. While these methods are still very effective, sometimes their adaption can be challenged due to today's postmodern culture.

The Romans Road method, for example, could be defined collectively as an intellectual evangelistic approach to sharing the gospel which uses a systematic methodology in expounding the plan of salvation through Bible verses found in the book of Romans. In this approach, the verses are organized into a simple teaching which is easy to itemize as an outline for anyone who is in need of salvation: why humanity needs salvation, the results of sin, how God provides that salvation, how a person can respond to God's provision of salvation, and finally what the result is of person's response to God's salvation.

The Romans Road method is advantageous in that it uses a biblically-based process and exposes the unconverted but biblically aware to Scripture. The message is focused around the understanding of scriptural reasoning rather than human logic. It is a popular evangelism method adopted by new Christians and experienced ones as well. The Romans Road can be a very effective method of reaching a person who recognizes the Bible as God's word and already willing to trust its teaching.

The disadvantage to this method comes when the non-Christian does not accept the Bible as the Word of God or an atheist who does not believe that God exists. Additionally, sometimes you can better explain the full extent of the gospel by using verses from throughout the bible instead of only Romans. Since this method is very straightforward, it doesn't specifically allow for any discussion. Sometimes, that can be interpreted by people as forcing ones' opinions, causing them to shut down, resisting anything you might be saying. The Romans Road is probably best used as a method to summarize the gospel in a concise fashion but it is not necessarily the best way to present the gospel in light of postmodern Christianity.

Another traditional method is called ***Evangelism Explosion*** (EE), which is a highly organized training method designed to reach non-Christians with the gospel. In this confrontational evangelistic method, the non-Christian is presented with a series of questions that emphasize the key points of the gospel and then they are challenged to respond. In training Christians to present the gospel, EE utilizes many framed questions such as "Do you know for sure that you are going to be with God in Heaven?" or "If God were to ask you, 'Why should I let you into My Heaven?' what would you say?"

The disadvantages to the EE method are two-fold. First, the training methods can result in autonomic dialogue. The evangelist memorizes questions, responses, and statements and begins to witness from a rehearsed script rather than engaging in a personal conversation with the person being witnessed to. This can result in the latter feeling like an experiment in a spiritual laboratory. The second disadvantage is that it can create false converts. When using this method as a high-pressure sales routine, the non-believer may give in to the pressure tactics because they feel backed into a corner but not because they are convicted by the Spirit.

Another popular method is known as the *Four Spiritual Laws*. Bill Bright in his book *Sharing the Abundant Life on Campus* elaborates regarding the Four Spiritual Laws:

> Begin a conversation on any appropriate subject and then turn the conversation to spiritual things. Talk about current world problems and ask if they see any likely solutions. They will ask you the same, which will enable you to share The Four Spiritual Laws and your personal testimony.

Bright then explains the need to "Listen carefully to the person with whom you are sharing your faith so that you can make specific applications for him in your presentation of The Four Spiritual Laws. Take hints from the things he says." Jard DeVille, from his book *The Psychology of Witnessing*, states that "It [Bright's method] is like rowing around an island, carefully studying the shoreline for an appropriate landing place. We explore our non-Christian friends' religious and family backgrounds, cultural interests, needs, dreams, and fears." This can be construed as deceptive and manipulative, since the witness is supposed to feign spontaneous interest in topics he or she otherwise would care nothing about.

It has been argued that the problem with the Four Spiritual Laws is that it is anthropocentric or "man-centered", implying that the pivotal issue is that an individual may know God's wonderful plan for his life. In each of the four laws there is mention of the Divine plan for a person's life. The story is as follows: God has a wonderful plan for our life; because of humankind's adverse spiritual condition we cannot know that plan for our life; when the proper steps are taken we can know the plan for our life.

In contrast, the biblical approach to evangelism is always theocentric or "God-centered." The authors of Scripture first laid the background about the being and attributes of God, sublime in His sovereignty, ineffable in His majesty and holiness. They highlighted that the righteousness of God has been revolted against by human sin and that if it were not for Divine grace, humanity's guilt (Rom. 3:19) would incur the wrath of God (Rom. 1:18), the deserved judgment of the Lord (Rom. 2:2), and ensuing death (Rom. 6:23).

The Navigators method called *The Bridge to Life* illustration has been an effective method of presenting/conceiving the gospel. It has been used to communicate the gospel successfully over many years and in many different contexts – in groups as well as by person-to-person.

The Bridge builds a "contractual" transaction. We recognize our "need." We receive Christ as the "solution." Then the "benefit" of this salvation is described. Next, there is an individual decision to "believe." At the conclusion, we pray this one prayer which guarantees me of eternal life. Revisions of this method add the need in terms of our broken relationship with God and the solution as a birth into a new relationship with God, which significantly improved the original version. Nonetheless, it still has its patented "If you've prayed this prayer and are trusting Christ, then the Bible says that you can be sure you have eternal life."

David Fitch, Betty R. Lindner Professor of Theology at Northern Seminary, commented on "The Bridge to Life" illustration:

> What's wrong with the Bridge's "transaction" approach? It has the effect of initiating the unbeliever into a salvation "for me" in the worst sense of those words. For in a consumerist society, the words "for me" can no longer mean what they meant when Paul spoke them or Luther spoke them. Consumerist society has trained all of us to think, feel and breathe all things as products to be consumed "for me." Jesus, Son of God, very God, has been reduced to an object to be used for some benefit.

[Traditional Evangelism Methods]

Additionally, The Bridge separates justification from sanctification. Although improvements have been made in the recent versions of The Bridge, salvation is still considered attained, end-point assured by confession. After praying the prayer, we now have the relationship as if it is already accomplished. The directions a convert is given to follow are individual exercises that hopefully keep them on the right path. They are not written as invitations into an endless expansive life with God and His Mission.

The largest contention with The Bridge illustration is that it takes no account for what happens to desire. The message leaves a convert to surmise that once they accept Christ's provision for sin and the separation from God, desire takes care of itself. They are instructed to read the Scriptures daily, pray often, witness to others, go to church and serve. These all appear to be individual exercises, which can easily turn into legalistic works to secure a life after conversion. But unless the re-formation of desire is addressed, these directions for the successful Christian life after conversion inevitably produce a failed Christian life and moral duplicity.

All in all, these discussed traditional methods can be used to approach a lost person with a pre-packaged message that assumes one scripted method fits all. The initiator approaches the "lost person" from a position of power as having the recipient's answer. They assume the questions to be asked and the answers that shall be given before they have even listened. The message is relayed intellectually and, more important, attitudinally. Those using these methods are saying with their presentation "we already know what the hell-bound sinner needs, what their problem is, and we're right and they're lost and confused." While this may be spiritually and positionally true, these traditional methods can completely alienate the listener and harden their hearts further against the message of salvation.

Evangelism for the sake of winning souls is not intrinsically centered on rehearsed techniques or scripted methods.

Spiritually-inspired evangelism wells up from a holy life and a surrendered heart, under the power of the Holy Spirit. The soul whose heart overflows with the witness of Christ is the intentional purpose of God. As Scripture says, apart from a holy life, none can see God (Heb. 12:14). While we walk in counsel with God's Spirit, we do not have to worry about what to say, for that which is to be said will be given to us the moment we speak (Mark 13:11). If we are abiding in the presence of God, out of our mouths will come life-giving healing (John 7:38), conviction and truth. Peter's words, when he preached, pierced the hearts of the listeners, but it was the Spirit that rent conviction that led to repentance. Christians are chosen tools in the hand of God. We must willingly submit every part of our lives to be used by God.

Traditional evangelistic strategies are not necessarily deficient in what they say, but in what they assume. These traditional methods have been effective for winning many souls to Christ, and we can be grateful that the Lord continues to use these methods. However, now that society has moved in a direction that is increasingly post-Christian, these methods cannot be considered the only possible approach. The presentation makes little sense unless presented within a religious framework in which the character of God is largely understood, the nature of sin is acknowledged, and the need for forgiveness is recognized. Unfortunately, in the post-Christian society in which we live people don't operate within these definitions. Evangelists today are looking for ways to hold together the propositional truth claims of Scripture and the grand narrative within which these claims find their meaning.

[3]
POSTMODERN EVANGELISM METHODS

Stepping beyond the traditional approach of evangelism is the postmodern reformed approach. We can look at a relatively new method coined by Steve Sjogren called **Servant Evangelism**, described by the motto "Small Things Done with Great Love Will Change the World." Sjogren has an article titled **94 Servant Evangelism Ideas for Your Church**. The ideas he lists are good and kind actions to do for your neighbors. The idea behind this relational evangelistic method is that Christians should reach people with love and compassion through service. The service should be provided with a vibrant heart, a generous attitude and an embracing smile. The mentality is that if service is done with the right attitude, the results will effectively lead people to a better appreciation of Christianity and draw them closer to accepting Jesus. Servant Evangelism is more about doing the message of the gospel rather than simply speaking it, and is popular in the postmodern emerging church.

The obvious disadvantage of the Servant Evangelism method is that it typically reduces the gospel to acts of kindness, philanthropy and social responsibility. It is not unusual for the layperson to conclude from this method that social services are the central tenets of evangelism due to the consumerist mindset promoted by the leadership of postmodern church. In servicing people's earthly needs, there can be a tendency by those receiving to never respond to the gospel, while being grateful for the kindness. This is not to say that we should only reach out to people if they are willing to respond to the message of salvation, but rather to balance the service with a clear presentation that mankind is sinful and in need of a Savior.

Another issue that can arise in Servant Evangelism is that once people reject the gospel, the servant evangelist is then faced with the persuasion to continue serving but without the gospel message. This is not a biblical conclusion and is not the same pattern as what is found in Jesus' ministry and defined commission. Within the context of evangelism, we are to share the gospel as the primary consideration, not to reduce it to social service methods supplemented by a sideline message. Within an evangelism context, Matt. 10:14 in part shows us if a person or people are not receptive to the message about Jesus, we are to move along to those who are. However, in our personal sphere, we are called to share the love and message of Christ with loved ones, co-workers and friends, praying that the Holy Spirit might transform their hearts, even if it takes many years.

Servant Evangelism, thus, is another method that is anthropocentric empowered by human efforts. Our good works do not demonstrate God's love, the crux of the gospel, but instead substitutes a lie for the truth. *"For God so loved the world, that he gave His only begotten Son"* (John 3:16) or *"Greater love hath no man than this that a man lay down his life for his friends"* (John 15:13). In all these Scriptures, we see God's love is shown to us through the death of His son for our sins. God's love is not manifested by our service to others nor is this service the essential catalyst of His love. In order for us to share God's love with another, it is ordained by God that we must tell how He gave His only son to die on the cross for our sins, without the postmodern ideology of social service supplanting the Gospel.

As times change, so do the approaches to people, but the message does not. God's message and methods never change, but changes in society do modify the comprehension of people. Today, one frequently hears about the emerging church offering possible strategies and new models for providing evangelism in a postmodern context – the postmodern attitude demands room for a spiritual conversation, but sometimes at the expense of the complete counsel of God.

Another postmodern method is called ***Relational Evangelism***, which emphasizes the kind of relationships we should develop with unbelievers; call it "friendship," "one-on-one" or "personal" evangelism. Other writers, stressing our attitude in these relationships, call it "contagious Christianity," "lifestyle evangelism" or "affinity evangelism." Regardless of what they call it, each concept title encourage us to become the kind of moral and friendly Christians that unbelievers want to be around.

How effective is relational evangelism? Evangelist Luis Palau's research shows that 75% of all those who come to Christ do so through a relationship by a saved friend, relative or co-worker. The Institute of American Church Growth reports an even higher percentage, with almost 90% of the 14,000 Christians recently polled saying they came to Christ through "a friend or relative who invested in a relationship with them." The details that we lack from these statistics are how many of these confessions result in a genuine relationship with Jesus, which include transformation? How many of these converts have left their former indulgences and worldly pursuits, who now have their hearts gaze fixed heavenward? With as many confessing Christians falling out the backdoor as coming in the front, it is clear that there is a great number who confess and conform to the social sphere of Christian gatherings, but who do not know Christ.

The push for a relational-model approach in evangelism and ministry within the modern Church is without a doubt a direct response to long-standing church culture that has over-valued traditional techniques which has become to be known as **propositionalism**. Younger leaders of the Gen X and Millennial generations in particular, view attempts to convert a person by way of intellectual assent and scriptural dialogue as inauthentic and manipulative. The solution, at least according to many, is to shift away from the intellectual and theological approach, towards a personal relationship.

While sometimes being profiled as egotistical, the observed problem with the current leaders in missions is not their sense of superiority, but rather their inclination towards the opposite extreme. Postmodernism has impacted missions in such a way that many missiologists want to remove the aggressive styles of evangelism that exploit the errors and inadequacies of other religions as they see it and replace it with "dialogue." They reason that this approach will minimize highlighting our differences with other religions instead of branding them as devilish counterfeits. This can be seen most visibly in what passes for Muslim missions in our day in the form of compromise documents such as *A Common Word between Us and You*, and in hyper-contextualizing approaches which almost seem ashamed to openly reveal the Christian's biblical position versus Islam.

Philosophies change and so do approaches. In the older generations, it is said that trust can only be violated; in the younger generations, trust can only be earned. Therefore it is surmised that if you are dealing with a group of people who are generally trusting and who value logic, even during the initial stages of acquaintance, then propositionalism would be a highly effective way to engage them for the purpose of sharing God's truth.

The problem lies in replacing the propositional evangelism with the relational; we have effectively perceived and employed relationship interaction as a technique. This categorically violates the very nature and sanctity of the motive behind the relationship. The moment we even acknowledge an intention to "use" a relationship for any purpose, it is no longer a relationship; it becomes a vehicle to a purposed end. This motivation fundamentally changes the way we view the other person, instead of a sinner needing grace, a person to skillfully befriend by honed behavior modification. It ultimately devalues them and it negates our integrity as manipulating for a religious purpose.

Jesus compels his disciples in Mark 12:31, saying *"You shall love your neighbor as yourself."* In Rom. 5:8, Paul describes how Christ provided the perfect model: *"But God shows his love for us in that while we were still sinners, Christ died for us."* Paul goes on to distill the nature of this love in Eph. 5:2, saying *"And walk in love, as Christ loved us and gave himself up for us a fragrant offering and sacrifice to God."* Love is characterized by what we offer, through what we received from God in Christ. Sustainable relationships depend on this principle and exist exclusive of any expectation of profit (spiritual or otherwise).

To clarify, relationship is absolutely critical to at least discipleship and the Christian community. But it is no more essential now than it ever has been. The primary complaint that members of older generations have against the relational approach is that it lacks scriptural substance. Since our culture has shifted towards distrust and skepticism, trust generally requires more time. Nevertheless, do we sacrifice the gospel presentation of Scripture for relational tactics or the philosophies behind them? No, I fear we have replaced God's wisdom with human wisdom by technique, claiming we have a better way. The message of Christ is not subject to loose effect to the epics of time, societies or cultures–it is the power to save; it is the timeless message to all generations.

We also must question the context of human philosophies revived within the religious community. We human beings are highly susceptible to *"exchanging the truth of God for a lie"* (see Rom. 1:18-25). Those who enter into evangelistic conversations with people living in our postmodern culture should train themselves in the humility of Christ, to speak in normal dialogue that is seasoned with Scripture, not with rehearsed methods or hidden manipulation tactics. We should realize that God's use of us is a knock upon the door, and we must wait until the Lord works upon the hearts of others in order for them to open themselves to the gospel. Above all, we must remember the cross of Christ as God's answer to our sin problem. The cross shows us how all our attempts are under judgment, but also how God responds to our hostility with redemption, to our guilt with grace, and to our resistance with love, all in the finished work of Jesus Christ.

Therefore, Evangelism is not a matter of delivering memorized speeches, nor is it dependent upon knowing the proper technique. In John Bowen's book *Evangelism for "Normal" People: Good News for Those Looking for a Fresh Approach* he writes, "The hunger for 'how-to' books, lectures, seminars, conferences, and media is the fruit of a particular modernist culture." This humanistic predisposition leads to mentalities such as: You can do it, simply try harder; You don't need help (apart from this method); You are competent (once you learn this method). It is this carnal understanding and attitude which has hampered the Holy Spirit's movement in the modern Church, and not least the God-ordained activity we call evangelism.

The tendency to draw a circle that defines insiders and outsiders and to try to persuade people to come inside by thinking "the way I do" is not helpful and it is not the way Jesus persuaded others. Scripture teaches us instead about the invitation Jesus made to His disciples in John 6:60-64 to have Him reside inside us. Few could accept that teaching in Jesus' day, probably even less today.

[4]
ASKING QUESTIONS IN EVANGELISM

One of the reasons that evangelists tend to overemphasize "coverage" over "engaged thinking" is that they assume that answers can be taught separate from questions. Instead of concentrating on posing statements or rehearsing scripted dialogue as is sometimes the case with traditional evangelism models, Christians should also learn to engage people in the way Jesus often did—by asking questions, even answering questions with questions. By using dialogue in this rabbinic style, we can engage people in such a way as to get them to think about their ideas and beliefs. Furthermore, and maybe more importantly, by doing so we can engage their hearts because a person's acceptance of the gospel is not solely based on their ability to reason. Asking questions can tear down entrenched strongholds of false views and build plausibility for the gospel.

Thinking is not driven by answers but by questions. Socrates was a Greek philosopher who taught by asking questions. When teachers ask questions that encourage listeners to draw their own conclusions, they are using the dialectic or "Socratic method" of teaching. Socrates concluded that while others professed knowledge they did not have, he knew how little he knew. In accepting his own ignorance, Socrates exemplifies the sort of humility that is essential to any rational inquiry. Also, in accepting his own ignorance, he accepts that there is a real difference between knowledge and mere opinion. Socrates asked many questions, however he provided few answers. He often denied knowing the answers to the questions he asked. The purpose of Socratic questioning is not to result in the acquisition of facts but rather to encourage people to think.

Jesus' use of questions was a part of His upbringing and cultural heritage. In fact, one snapshot we have of His early life involves Him sitting in the Temple courts at the age of twelve asking questions of the city's religious elders (Luke 2:41-52). So, clearly this was a skill which He honed from His early years. Toward the end of Mark's Gospel (Mark 12:35-37) we read of an encounter Jesus had later in His life with other religious elders in which He proposed a classical Jewish question, called a ***Haggadah*** question. A Haggadah question is one which tries to reconcile two biblical ideas which seem to contradict or at least be opposed to one another. And in so doing, Jesus pushed His listeners to come to grips with who He really was and His divine purpose.

When we consider the questions that Jesus asks we are impressed by the wisdom they contain and how skilfully they identify the important details of life. Thus when He challenged each individual from among the multitude and those who were already disciples to *"deny himself, and take up his cross, and follow me"* (Mark 8:34), He points out the reason for this choice by using two questions: *"For what shall it profit a man, if he shall gain the whole world, and lose his own soul?"*; and, *"Or what shall a man give in exchange for his soul?"* (vv. 36, 37). These questions make the point that the gift of life is essential to everything that we have and experience. Consequently, to grasp prematurely what we desire without regard to God's requirements is at best only of short-term value.

Many of the questions Jesus asked came from encounters with the authorities, who opposed His teaching and rejected His call to repentance and their need to recognize that He was from God. Early in Mark's record, Jesus reveals His insight into His opponents' thinking: *"And immediately Jesus, perceiving in His spirit that they thus questioned within themselves, said to them, "Why do you question these things in your hearts? Which is easier, to say to the paralytic, 'Your sins are forgiven,' or to say, 'Rise, take up your bed and walk'?"* (Mark 2:8-9). They believed that physical infirmity was the consequence of sin (see John 8:34 and context), therefore the subsequent healing of the palsied man gave incontrovertible evidence that Jesus had been given the authority to forgive sins, even though they refused to accept His office and divinity.

Asking questions will help us understand what is in a person's heart and mind. That is what Jesus did, and we find Him taking this approach repeatedly in His discussions with people. In Matt. 6:28 He asked, *"Why are you anxious about clothing?"* In Matt. 7:3 He asked, *"Why do you see the speck that is in your brother's eye, but do not notice the log that is in your own eye?"* A page or two later in Matt. 8:26, His question was, *"Why are you afraid, O you of little faith?"* In Matt. 9:4, we read of an encounter with His opponents where Jesus, *"knowing their thoughts, said, 'Why do you think evil in your hearts?'"* Similarly in Matt. 22:18: *"But Jesus, aware of their malice, said, 'Why put me to the test, you hypocrites?'"* Jesus was not asking out of confusion or even curiosity. He knew their thoughts; He knew what was going on under the surface. He wasn't asking because he needed to know. He was asking questions in order for the hearer to inevitably teach themselves through introspection. He was, in fact, urging his followers and foes to peer below the surface, inviting them to think about what they were doing and whether it really made sense.

One of the most mysterious series questions asked in Scripture was when Jesus asked Peter *"Do you love me?"* as recorded in John 21:15-17. This occurred when Jesus was having breakfast with His disciples soon after His resurrection. Jesus used this opportunity to encourage and exhort Peter about his upcoming responsibilities and even prophesies the manner in which Peter will die. By asking Peter *"do you love me?"* three times, Jesus was emphasizing the importance of Peter's love and unswerving obedience to his Lord as necessary for his future ministry. Each time

Peter answers in the affirmative, Jesus follows up with the command for Peter to feed His sheep. His meaning is that if Peter truly loves his Master, he is to shepherd and care for those who belong to Christ. His words reveal Peter's role as the leader of the new Church, the Body of Christ in Jerusalem that would be responsible for spreading the gospel after Jesus' ascension into heaven.

It has been suggested that by His repeated question Jesus is subtly reminding Peter of his three denials that took place as Jesus was being led away to appear before the Sanhedrin, Pilate and Herod, and later crucified. However, a better explanation exists. The Koine Greek sheds light on what is normally unknown about the original words used. When Jesus asked Peter *"do you love me?"* in John 21:15-16, He used the Greek word *agape* which refers to unconditional love. Both times, Peter responded with *"Yes, Lord; you know that I love you,"* using the Greek word *phileo* which refers more to a brotherly/friendship type of love. It would seem that Jesus is trying to get Peter to understand that he must love Jesus unconditionally in order to be the leader God is calling him to be. The third time Jesus asks *"do you love me?"* in John 21:17, He uses the word *phileo*, and Peter again responds with *"Lord, you know everything; you know that I love you,"* again using *phileo*. The point in the different Greek words for love seems to be that Jesus was pressing Peter to move him from *phileo* love to *agape* love.

Jesus only directly answers 3 of the 183 questions that He himself is asked in the four gospels. This takes traditional Christians by surprise, which have been taught to assume that the very purpose of evangelism is to give people answers and to resolve their spiritual dilemmas. Jesus either keeps silent as with Pilate (John 19:9), returns with another question as with the coin of Caesar (Matt. 22:19), or gives an illustration, as with the Good Samaritan story (Luke 10:30f).

At other times, Jesus returns the question back inside the frame of reference of the inquirer, as if to critique it. He does so with the rich young ruler: *"You know the commandments"* (Mark 10:19). Sometimes Jesus can only weep, sigh, or lament because of the seeming malevolence represented in the question, as when the Pharisees ask for a sign from Him (Mark 8:12). Here He refuses to respond. He had learned that any attempt to interact with an entrenched position of resentment or ego-fortified suspicion would normally only be used to dig the trench deeper and further secure the argument. Many times, silence, quiet prayer and genuine love for the opponent are the best answers, even though you will be judged harshly in the moment and by any observers.

If we can understand this basic dynamic, perhaps we can see what Jesus is doing in asking His own questions. Jesus' questions are meant to challenge us, force us to examine our unconscious biases, free us from our dualistic mindsets, challenge our narrow view of God or value placed upon the world. He himself does not usually expect specific answers. His questions are worth examining because they, along with the parables, reveal His basic style of encounter with the soul, or what we would call today, His style of "evangelization."

C.S. Lewis addresses this very issue in his essay on Christian Apologetics in his collection of essays **God in the Dock**:

> We can make people attend to the Christian point of view for half an hour or so, but the moment they have gone away from our lecture or laid down our article, they are plunged back into a world where the opposite position is taken for granted. As long as that situation exists, widespread success is simply impossible.

This is the final anemia of any religion based primarily on sermons rather than a change of heart that leads to a relationship with God. What is needed is genuine love and concern for the persons we encounter, asking questions because we truly desire to know the person, and prayer for the discernment of the Holy Spirit about what to say.

Jesus always reminds us that *"God alone is good"* (Mark 10:18) and we had best not try to create our own goodness by providing ourselves with rehearsed or immediate answers about great and intentionally unanswerable questions. Jesus merely lists the memorized commandments to a young inquiring man, while cleverly and compassionately slipping in "Do not defraud" second to the last. He does not really answer his self-reassuring question about "What must I do to inherit eternal life?" but instead quietly reveals the likely sin of this rich young man. Jesus knows how he obtained his wealth, and that is why He dares to tell him that he must give it all away: *"His face fell and he went away"* (Mark 10:22). The young man wanted to think of himself as good instead of rejoicing in the goodness of God. This is the problem with any religion based primarily on morality and satisfying answers, instead of questions. As a result, he missed the primary call, the moment of sheer relationship, the ultimate questioning of the soul, when *"Jesus looked steadily at him and loved him."*

[5]
OPEN-AIR EVANGELISM

Open-air evangelism or street preaching is literally what it says, evangelizing in the open air in public places and on street corners. Considering the heritage of open-air preaching recorded throughout Church history, why don't we hear more of it today? John the Baptist was an open-air preacher, as was Jesus, Paul and Peter. Jesus preached arguably the greatest sermon of all time called the "Sermon on the Mount" in the open-air. Peter preached in the open-air at Pentecost and Paul chose to stand on Mars Hill and preach open-air to the Athenians. Stephen did so in Acts 7 and many other biblical characters such as Jeremiah, Amos, Jotham, Jonah, and Isaiah were all open-air preachers.

Early preachers such as John Wesley, George Whitefield, D. L. Moody, General William Booth, and R. A. Torrey all preached in public places, which allowed them to attract crowds larger than most buildings could accommodate. Charles Haddon Spurgeon spoke at great length about the subject, and his thoughts are of added value to this chapter. He stated once in expressing the value of open-air preaching, "It would be very easy to prove that revivals of religion have usually been accompanied, if not caused, by a considerable amount of preaching out of doors, or in unusual places." From his book ***Lectures to My Students***, a source of reference many pastors cherish, we find these words of support and defense:

> I fear that in some of our less enlightened country churches there are conservative individuals who almost believe that to preach anywhere except in the chapel would be a shocking innovation, a sure token of heretical tendencies, and a mark of zeal without knowledge. Any young brother who studies his comfort among

them must not suggest anything as irregular as a sermon outside the walls of their Zion. In the olden times we are told, "Wisdom crieth without, she uttereth her voice in the streets, she crieth in the chief places of concourse, in the openings of the gates"; but the wise men of orthodoxy would have wisdom gagged except beneath the roof of a licensed building. These people believe in a New Testament which says, "Go out into the highways and hedges and compel them to come in," and yet they dislike a literal obedience to the command.

Charles Spurgeon continues,

> No sort of defense is needed for preaching out of doors; but it would need very potent arguments to prove that a man had done his duty who has never preached beyond the walls of his meeting-house. A defense is required rather for services within buildings than for worship outside of them. The great benefit of open-air preaching is that we get so many new comers to hear the gospel who otherwise would never hear it. The street evangelist, moreover, wins attention from those eccentric people whose religion can neither be described nor imagined. Such people hate the very sight of our churches and meeting houses, but will stand in a crowd to hear what is said, and are often most impressed when they affect the greatest contempt.

In Matt. 10:27, Jesus gave an order to His apostles saying, *"What I tell you in darkness that speak ye in light, and what ye hear in the ear, that preach ye upon the housetops."* His apostles continued to carry out His command in the book of Acts. On the day of Pentecost, we find one of the greatest examples of open-air preaching written in the New Testament. In Acts 2:14, Peter utilized the delivery method of open-air preaching at the beginning of the Church age.

While the Old Testament is typically not referenced for evangelism in context with the new covenant, we can find plenty of examples. Jeremiah, for example, was a bold open air street preacher: *"The word that came to Jeremiah from the Lord, saying, Stand in the <u>gate</u> of the Lord's house, and <u>proclaim there this word</u>, and say, Hear the word of the*

[OPEN-AIR EVANGELISM]

Lord, all ye of Judah, that enter in at these gates to worship the Lord" (Jeremiah 7:1-2).

Further on we read, *"Then the Lord said unto me, Proclaim all these words in the cities of Judah, and in the streets of Jerusalem, saying, Hear ye the words of this covenant, and do them"* (Jeremiah 11:6).

Found recorded in the book of Judges 9:7, we learn that Jotham had a message to deliver to a crowd of people who wanted to kill him in Shechem. How did he do it? Jotham *"went and stood in the top of Mount Gerizim, and lifted up his voice, and cried, and said unto them, Hearken unto me, ye men of Shechem, that God may hearken unto you."* Jotham found an elevated place from which all could hear him, and yelled loudly with intensity. Jotham was an open-air preacher circa 1300 B.C.

In Ezra 10:9-14, Ezra called the people of Israel to repentance as they sat in the open. *"Then all the men of Judah and Benjamin assembled at Jerusalem within the three days. It was the ninth month, on the twentieth day of the month. And all the people sat in the open square before the house of God, trembling because of this matter and because of the heavy rain."* The word translated "square" or "bir·hō·wb" in Hebrew, means any broad open space, and is probably used here to designate the great court of the temple. By *"all the people"* we may understand as many as the court would conveniently hold. If the court had the dimensions given it by Greek historian and sceptic philosopher Hecataeus of Abdera, it may have accommodated all the Jews in that country, which is a phenomenal consideration.

Another classic example was God sending Jonah to warn Nineveh. Jonah was charged to preach to Nineveh, not only to those who would attend his meeting, but to the whole city. The Bible reports that Nineveh was *"an exceeding great city of three days journey"* (Jonah 3:3), meaning it took three days to walk through it. Greek historian Diodorus Siculus verifies this by recording that Nineveh was 60 miles in circumference.

[FINDING THE BALANCE IN WORLD MISSIONS]

Jonah 3:4 goes on to report that *"Jonah began to enter into the city a day's journey, and he cried [shouted], and said, Yet forty days, and Nineveh shall be overthrown."* He was preaching as he was walking outdoors, to strangers without technique or strategy, simply empowered by and under the direction of God.

A historic example of proponents of open-air preaching was the Franciscan Order in the Catholic Church, founded by Francis of Assisi (1182-1226). Francis was an open-air street preacher, later revered by Catholics and Protestants alike for his dedication to a biblical Evangelical Christianity. He was the son of a wealthy cloth merchant and spent his youth in pleasure and frolicking until he became a prisoner of war and fell ill. This experience caused him to reflect on eternity. He later took seriously the commands of Christ to His disciples to sell all and give to the poor, which Francis and his followers did, and received permission from the Pope for their order "to preach repentance everywhere." According to the Catholic Encyclopedia (1909), Francis "usually preached out of doors, in the market-places, from church steps, from the walls of castle courtyards."

Another example of Franciscan zeal is shown by the service of Berard of Carbio, a frair of the Franciscan Order by St. Francis of Assisi. He was sent with four other monks named Peter, Otho, Accursius, and Adjutus to preach the gospel to the Mohammedans (a term for a follower of the Islamic prophet Muhammad) of the West in 1219. The five missionaries set sail from Italy and landed in Seville, then still under Muslim rule, where their preaching proved fruitless. After sojourning some time in Spain and Portugal, they traveled to the Kingdom of Morocco. Despite the fact that the only one of the five who knew any Arabic was Berard, their open preaching of the gospel and their bold denunciation of Islam soon caused them to be considered insane. However, when it became apparent that they would neither go away nor stop preaching, they were apprehended

[OPEN-AIR EVANGELISM]

and cast into prison. Having with effort, vainly endeavored to persuade them to abandon their faith to Jesus Christ, the Moorish king Abu Yaqub Yusuf II, in a fit of rage, beheaded them with his scimitar, making them the first martyrs of the Franciscan Order.

A lesser known historic example was The Waldensians, who were purportedly founded by Peter Waldo, a wealthy merchant in Lyons, France in the 12th century. The story goes that one day he asked a theologian what he should do to gain eternal life. He was answered with the words of Jesus to the rich young ruler, to sell his possessions, give the money to the poor, and follow Christ. Waldo took this literally, selling his business, giving away his wealth. He and his followers traveled by twos, preaching in the streets, reading passages of Scripture which they translated themselves into the common language. Pope Alexander III, while impressed with their tenets of poverty and assisting the poor, forbade them from preaching or providing any explanation or critical interpretation (exegesis) without authorization from the local clergy. Despite this admonition, Waldo and his followers continued to preach in public, declaring instead that they "must obey God rather than man."

In the 1730s, a devote man from Christian history, John Wesley headed to Herrnhut, the Moravian headquarters in Germany, to study. Though he met the Fetter Lane Society, along with other religious organizations, and published a collection of hymns for them, the gates of parish churches remained closed, when it came to preaching. It was not until his Oxford friend George Whitefield's first preaching in the open air, to a company of miners, that John gave his first sermon in a public place near Bristol. Though the idea of preaching in the open air seemed more a sin than a practice, this thought was soon dissolved.

John Wesley wrote in his journal,

> Saturday, 31 March, 1731. In the evening I reached Bristol, and met Mr. Whitefield there. I could scarce reconcile myself at first

to this strange way of preaching in the fields, of which he set me an example on Sunday; having been all my life (till very lately) so tenacious of every point relating to decency and order, that I should have thought the saving of souls almost a sin, if it had not been done in a church.

Such were the feelings of a man who posthumously came to be considered one of the greatest open-air preachers that ever lived.

John Wesley later wrote:

> I am persuaded that the more open-air preaching there the better; if it becomes a nuisance to be a blessing to others—if properly conducted. If the gospel is spoken, and if the spirit of the preacher is one of love and truth, the results cannot be doubted: The bread cast upon the waters must be found after many days. (See Eccles. 11:1.) At the same time, it must be the gospel, and it must be preached in a manner worth the hearing, for mere noisemaking is an evil rather than a benefit.

Despite all the popular evangelism methods used, it might surprise some Christians to learn that there is not an emphasis on "one-on-one" witnessing found in Scripture. There are only three recorded occasions in Jesus' ministry where one-on-one witnessing is mentioned: Nicodemus (John 2:13-3:1), the woman at the well (John 4), and Zaccheus (Luke 19:1-5). Overall, the gospels spend much more time documenting Christ's messages to "multitudes" (examples: Matt. 4:25; 5:1; 8:1; 18; 12:15; 13:2,34; 14:14; 15:10,30-35,39; 17:14; 19:2; 21:8,11).

This chapter would not be complete without quoting Charles Haddon Spurgeon again from his book *Lectures to My Students. Volume 3, Lecture IV, Open-Air Preaching—A Sketch of its History* which provides a glimpse into the open-air preaching times of Spurgeon.

> It was a blessed day when Methodists and others began to proclaim Jesus in the open air; then were the gates of hell shaken, and the captives of the devil set free by hundreds and by thousands. Once recommenced, the fruitful agency of field-

[OPEN-AIR EVANGELISM]

preaching was not allowed to cease. Amid jeering crowds and showers of rotten eggs and filth, the immediate followers of the two great Methodists [Whitefield & Wesley] continued to storm village after village and town after town. Very varied were their adventures, but their success was generally great. One smiles often when reading incidents in their labours. A string of packhorses is so driven as to break up a congregation, and a fire-engine is brought out and played over the throng to achieve the same purpose. Hand-bells, old kettles, marrow-bones and cleavers, trumpets, drums, and entire bands of music were engaged to drown the preachers' voices. In one case the parish bull was let loose, and in others dogs were set to fight. The preachers needed to have faces set like flints, and so indeed they had. John Furz says: "As soon as I began to preach, a man came straight forward, and presented a gun at my face; swearing that he would blow my brains out, if I spake another word. However, I continued speaking, and he continued swearing, sometimes putting the muzzle of the gun to my mouth, sometimes against my ear. While we were singing the last hymn, he got behind me, fired the gun, and burn off part of my hair." After this, my brethren, we ought never to speak of petty interruptions and annoyances. The proximity of a blunderbuss in the hands of a son of Belial is not very conducive to collected through and clear utterance, but the experience of Furz was probably no worse than that of John Nelson, who coolly says, "But when I was in the middle of my discourse, one at the outside of the congregation threw a stone, which cut me on the head : however, that made the people give greater attention, especially when they saw the blood running down my face; so that all was quiet till I had done, and was singing a hymn.

As mentioned in other parts of this book, the traditional understanding of evangelism is an office that has been assigned to the leaders in the Church. In addition to this, the understanding of evangelism has been defined as conversing, witnessing, sharing, or a relationship. These modern methods, for all practical purposes, virtually eliminate or replace the need for the open-air evangelism highlighted in Scripture. Unfortunately, contemporary "definitions" can potentially distract those who might take the time to read, comprehend and follow the examples found in the Bible.

Indeed, Scripture is adamant that we all have different gifts, and should operate within them as the Lord gives us grace. In Acts 2, Peter was operating in accordance with the natural temperament that was bestowed by God upon him. He was bold, forward, ardent, and he rose to defend the apostles of Jesus Christ, and Christ Himself, from an injurious charge. Not daunted by ridicule or opposition, he felt that now was the time for preaching the gospel to the crowd that had been assembled by curiosity.

While we are all gifted according to our own propensity and wisdom of God, we are all earnestly charged to share the gospel by whatsoever means, manner or capacity we may have. This charge may entail boldly speaking to a crowd, discussing in private with a friend, or sharing the good news amidst an assembly of believers.

[6]
SPIRITUALITY AROUND THE WORLD

While this chapter might seem unrelated to world missions, it has everything to do with what is encountered in missions and evangelism. A brief reflection on historical Christianity, ending with a partial panoramic view of current faith-trends and modern thought is vital to serving in missions with comprehension.

Many different types of spirituality have grown from the original Christian faith, including a whole range of traditions from antiquity. It is part of modern thought and thus part of a wide-ranging 19th century transformation, a historical rupture called the Great Transformation, which included Industrial Revolution of the late eighteenth and early nineteenth centuries. As such, it is part of a "cognitive globalization," a political, economic, and cultural integration of the world. This integration is uneven in time and place, and occurs at different levels of society, integrating markets, political systems and religious thought.

There exist many different schools of spirituality which developed in different countries during different periods of history. The list might include faiths such as Christianity, Judaism, Buddhism, Hinduism, Islam, the Zoroastrian religion and the Native American religions or any number of faiths. Among them you will find something in common: namely, the quest of the human spirit for something that is bigger, deeper, "more than" the limits of the physical life.

All humanity shares an inner longing for reunification with the Creator, although often incorrectly identified or pursued in a misguided manner. Isaiah expressed this well when he wrote, *"My soul yearns for you in the night; in the morning my spirit longs for you"* (Isaiah 26:9a). Ultimately, we are intrinsically made for the eternal and therefore cannot be ultimately satisfied by the temporal. Scripture reflects this longing from the passage, *"God has set eternity in the hearts of men"* Eccl. 3:11.

The very existence of different types highlights the historical diversity of human religious comprehension and activity, the widely varying responses to the discovery and unfolding of the spirit, the ever new, creative responses of faith to different experiences. This diversity also demonstrates that there is no single universal spirituality, not even within one religious tradition. There are many unique "spiritualties" linked to specific times and places, to different socio-political-economic conditions, and to different forms of awareness, even though it may ultimately belong to the single essence of spirituality to transcend the contingencies of all of these.

In the past, much of Christian spirituality was developed by a social, cultural and intellectual elite which alone had the leisure for cultivating mind and spirit, for developing an alternative to the dominant culture of their times. For Catholics the predominant method of sanctification was the cloister, a separation from mainstream society by insertion into an alternative parallel community. With the rise of Protestantism the method of sanctification shifted from the cloister to the ordinary life in the world with its day-to-day relationships and responsibilities. Spiritual formation was no longer pursued in separate institutions but occurred in the world at large. A new spirituality developed which was not without precedents, found in earlier Christian teaching.

The history of Christianity chronicles the parallel existence of two models of spirituality: the ascetic/monastic model of renunciation spirituality and the model of what might be called the "householder spirituality," a spirituality of living in the world, a concept taken from Indian religions where both of these models are also present. In Islam and Judaism only the latter is known, whereas during much of Christian history the former was dominant.

[SPIRITUALITY AROUND THE WORLD]

At this point we might ask, "Are the past models of spirituality appropriate or adequate for contemporary culture?" In terms of the diversity of spiritual practice and of the understanding of spirituality today, there is no doubt that there are strong historical links with the past, but also a number of discontinuities. We have to deal with a new order of modern complexity, not only in our culture but also in the understanding and practice of spirituality.

A study, supported by a grant from the John Templeton Foundation, provides a summary of international data from around the world, which reveals several patterns of spirituality and religiosity among young adults. One is the relationship between a country's level of economic development and the spirituality and religiosity of its population. As countries develop economically, there is less emphasis on dominant religious traditions and values and more emphasis placed on secular institutions, as well as educational and economic accomplishment, powered by the need for trained workforces in industrialized societies.

Another pattern is the clear imprint of religion on beliefs in countries with a history of an influential religious tradition, such as Islam or Catholicism, so that young adults from these countries score relatively high on questions of spirituality and religious thought. Likewise, there is an imprint of the secular traditions of communist, socialist, and welfare states, reflected in the low importance given to religion and God in countries of the former Soviet Union, where religion was suppressed and atheism was promoted by the state and widely adopted by citizens, including the Nordic welfare states. In addition, formerly Confucian societies (Japan, China) have a tradition of secular bureaucratic authority that is reflected in the low importance attached to God and religion in those countries as well.

Many in the West who identify themselves as Christian do so only superficially. These "cultural Christians" use the term "Christian" but do not practice the faith. Christian nominalism is not a new trend. As soon as any belief system is broadly held in a culture, people are motivated to adopt it, even with minimal connection. Yet, much of the change in our religious identification is in nominal Christians, who no longer use the term and, instead, do not identify with any religion. In other words, the nominal are becoming the unidentified. Despite these cultural transitions, Christianity continues as it is amalgamated by society. Studies such as the General Social Survey show that the evangelical movement has remained generally steady from 1972 to today.

While there is interest in spirituality in almost every region in the world, there are many people who describe themselves with the words of the title of a recent book: ***Spiritual, But Not Religious*** (SBNR), which is a popular phrase, a synonym used to self-identify a life stance of spirituality that rejects traditional, organized religion as the sole or most valuable means of furthering spiritual growth. Those of this sentiment see themselves as open to "spiritual" matters, but they identify "religion" and the external propagation of evangelism as an undesirable facet found within the organized Church.

A growing number of those who used to define themselves as Christian have relegated their previous credentials and now embrace nature worship. The Finnic people called Estonians, for example, were recently asked whether religion played an important part in their life, and only 20% of the surveyed population said "yes." This suggests that the Baltic country is, statistically, the least religious country in the world. Some Estonians consider themselves spiritual. One man defined his religion as Maausk—a form of Estonian nature spirituality—in which the trees and earth are cherished objects that possess power. Among their numbers, well over 50% of Estonians say they do believe in a spirit or life force, however vaguely defined.

There is a definable spiritual metamorphosis occurring in the West. For example, some former Christians have progressively become Pantheist. Books like ***When God Is Gone,***

[SPIRITUALITY AROUND THE WORLD]

Everything Is Holy: The Making of a Religious Naturalist by Chet Raymo helps propagate this trend. Pantheists do not believe in a distinct personal or anthropomorphic god. Some eastern religions have highlighted the importance of pantheism, most notably Hinduism and Taoism. However, the very essence of Christianity refutes pantheism. Christian scripture states that God created everything, not that he is everything or that everything is God. While Christianity teaches that God is omnipresent, or exists everywhere, it separates the Creator from his creations.

Another growing identification among Christians is called Progressive (postmodern) Christianity or Christian agnosticism, where a Christian agnostic claims to be Christian despite uncertainty about whether Christian teachings are true. They surmise that it is not possible to know for certain if God exists. Faith and doubt are often seen as antagonistic, but they perceive them as complimentary – they coexist in tension, where without one there would not be the other.

A Christian agnostic accepts the Bible as a collection of books written over a 1,000-year timeframe. As such, the Scriptures represent a conversation with and about God, with God as the central conversation partner. However, since the people who wrote the Bible were working within the cultures and worldviews of their day, the Christian agnostic is unlikely to view the Bible as inerrant. This stands in contrast to the conservative view that the Bible is a divine monologue written by God, inerrant not only in theology but in history and science as well. The Christian agnostic tries to understand the dynamics of the conversations happening within the Bible, and to engage these conversations. Many Bible stories are understood not literally, but as parables.

On the contrary, conservative Christianity is bound to knowing God through presuppositions. Hence the creeds, the statements of faith, the doctrinal statements, and other historical writings are foundational to many long-standing denominations. For this way of knowing God, belief is central. One must believe in God because God cannot be known through experience, only by faith. For many progressive/emerging Christians, beliefs about God are not considered central. Rather, God is known through experience. And for many in transition or emerging, this experience of knowing God comes through knowing Jesus experientially. To experience the person of Jesus is, on some level, to experience God himself. Experience supersedes faith, and humanistic ideals amalgamate with post-Christian ideologies, where the Church emerges as a new social order less its historic formalisms.

Atheism continues to grow rapidly in the West, clarifying the Scripture, *"Let no man deceive you by any means: for that day shall not come, except there come a falling away first"* 2 Thess. 2:3. Between 1.5 and 4 percent admit to so-called "hard atheism," the conviction that no higher power exists. But a much larger share of the American public (19 percent) spurns organized religion in favor of a non-defined skepticism about faith. This group, sometimes collectively labeled the "Nones," is growing faster than any religious faith in the West. About two thirds of Nones say they are former believers; 24 percent are lapsed Catholics and 29 percent once identified with other Christian denominations. In the United States alone, Ameroatheists have grown by 10 million since the turn of the century—representing about a million a year, and about a third of overall population growth, to a total of 60 million out of more than 300 million. Atheism has made large gains among the young, while congregation size has dropped by as much as a fifth.

Atheist, Gnostic, Theist, Agnostic as four labels on a halved square can be very useful in describing the way post-Christian people feel about God. They can combine together to make more precise labels:
- An atheist agnostic is someone who does not believe in gods and also thinks that the existence of gods cannot be known. This might mean that they don't believe

in gods because they haven't seen any evidence that supports their existence.
- A theist gnostic is someone who believes in a god or gods and thinks that the existence of gods can be known. This position is usually referred to as just "theist", since people who believe in gods, usually also think that their existence can be known.
- An atheist gnostic is someone who does not believe in gods, and who thinks that we can know that gods do not exist. A fairly unusual position, they might think they have found proof of the non-existence of gods, or might have been persuaded by life experiences.
- A theist agnostic is someone who believes in gods, but thinks that they could not know for sure that their god exists. Another fairly unusual position, as people who have faith in gods typically also think that their god can be known to be real.

Dr. Paul Visser is the pastor of a congregation in The Hague, the Netherlands. On the basis of his extensive experience in a postmodern European context, he recently provided a helpful perspective on evangelism efforts. He not only presented new possibilities for evangelistic outreach, but also cautioned us that this reawakening of spirituality is not always positive. He wrote:

> We are separated from God because of our sin and rebellion. Human beings have turned against God with the idea that they can be gods themselves. In the depths of their being they no longer want to know about God. In the secularized West many have taken radical leave of God without any sense that they are missing anything.

He goes on to say:

> But God is not separated from us. Although people may no longer overtly seek after God, in their emptiness they are continually searching for themselves, asking the fundamental questions: Who am I? (for identity); What must I do? (for

guidance); How do I escape? (for help); What is my purpose in life? (for meaning). The unbeliever senses that there must be more to life than a flat empirical reality. This sense is the notion of God, a religious consciousness that comes from God who reveals himself through his general revelation.

Keeping in mind these observations, we can note that the postmodern situation does bring about new possibilities for evangelistic and missions outreach. If we want to fulfill our evangelistic task in a relevant and adequate way we must accept the other person from their perspective and attempt to understand their source of inspiration; any attitude of having the only truth will certainly be a barrier to our witness. The leaders of the post-modern church movement have something to teach us about this sensitivity. At the same time, we need to do more than simply be sensitive to the person and his or her culture. Perhaps at this point the emerging church tends to be as captive to postmodern culture as it accuses the modern church of being captive to modernity. Reformed evangelism teaches us to look at the spiritual dynamics behind what we see in our culture and evaluate them in light of Scripture.

[7]
THE CHALLENGE OF SYNCRETISM

Syncretism in relation to missions is important to understand. Both in the history of its usage, and in contemporary usage, the word syncretism has had varied meanings. It is generally defined by anthropologists as the combining of different (often seemingly contradictory) beliefs, while melding practices of various schools of thought. Syncretism may involve the merger of several originally discrete traditions, especially in the theology and mythology of religion, thus asserting an underlying unity and allowing for an inclusive approach to other faiths.

Religious syncretism specifically, is the blending of two or more religious belief systems into a new system, or the incorporation of beliefs from unrelated traditions into a revised religious tradition, which on the surface seems very attractive to the adherents of various groups. This can occur for many reasons, and the latter scenario happens quite commonly in areas where multiple religious traditions exist in proximity and function actively in the culture, or when a culture is conquered, and the conquerors bring their religious beliefs with them, but do not succeed in entirely eradicating the old beliefs or practices.

There are a number of theologians with a progressive bent – those who have studied, and are open to or have been influenced by the social sciences, especially cultural anthropology – who view syncretism as positive, often approaching it more from the anthropological rather than the theological perspective. It is for them a necessary stage in the process of inculturation, the process by which a person adapts to and assimilates the culture in which he or she lives. They view syncretism as inevitable and necessary for the growth, development, and enrichment of the church and its doctrines. They therefore do not comprehend any religious compromise or inconsistent eclecticism.

Harvie M. Conn, from his 1984 book, ***Eternal Word and Changing Worlds***, discusses the problematic context. He states that syncretism occurs "...when critical and Basic Elements of the Gospel are lost in the process of contextualization and are replaced by religious elements from the receiving culture, there is a synthesis with this partial Gospel." Conn also refers to a theological declaration which calls syncretism an "uncritical affirmative approach to the evaluation of eastern religions and cultures," and "the unjustifiable fusion of irreconcilable tenets and practices."

Indian Theologian Joseph Prasad Pinto, OFMCap (Order of Friars Minor Capuchin), from his book ***Inculturation Through Basic Communities***, refers to a common definition as the "fusion of incompatible elements" or the "mingling authentic notions and realities of the revealed faith with realities of other spiritual worlds." A culture borrows elements of another religion, without critically passing them through the screen of Christianity. Hence Christianity is watered down or destroyed in this process. This same concern was expressed by the Council Fathers during Vatican II, stating that true Christianity will not be nourished by such syncretism, but rather diluted or destroyed.

Theologians such as British Bishop James Edward Lesslie Newbigin (1909-1998) speak of the Neopaganism of the West. He expressed in 1987, with many others, that Western Christianity has been overpowered by the values and disvalues of the modern world. Modern culture is resistant to the gospel message. Christians too easily identify with contemporary Western culture, and lose the ability to be critical in light of the gospel. We are guided less and less by Christian principles, and more and more by secular and even pagan values. He remarks that a new, negative syncretism between Christianity and modern culture has been forged

[THE CHALLENGE OF SYNCRETISM]

and that the future of Christianity is at stake. A few examples where this might be true is in the increasing denial of the doctrine of hell, increased divorce rates among Christians and Catholics, as well as denial of the reality of the devil or evil spirits in first world nations.

Syncretism has been affecting Christian evangelism and missions since the first century, altering Christian practices through cultural accommodation so that they consciously or unconsciously blend with those of the dominant culture. This is similar to how the early Christian Church stretched across Europe during the time of Constantine, absorbing many of the pagan traditions from the cultures it dominated in regards to ritualism, symbolism, deities, etc. Many religions as they expand tend to adapt themselves to time and place. Although some have tried to use these examples to argue that religion is a human invention and tool for political manipulation, this is not always the case. On the contrary, this phenomenon among cultures could also depict the universality of belief in a higher intelligence and ever evolving search for truth among all civilizations.

Religious syncretism can be intentionally developed through relational evangelism when it attempts to make its message and life-style attractive, alluring, and appealing to those outside the faith. Over a period of years the accommodations become routine, integrated into the narrative story of the Christian community and inseparable from its definition. When major worldview changes occur within the dominant culture, the Church has difficulty separating the eternal from the temporal. The Church tends to lose her moorings because she has for too long been swept along with the cultural currents. Syncretism thus occurs when Christianity transitions into the main cultural compositions of its society.

Syncretism is caused by many things, not the least being poor communication. For missionaries to communicate clearly, it helps to have a proficient working knowledge of the language and culture. Though this can hardly be mandatory in all situations, an understanding of the problems that develop when using second or trade languages is critical (A trade language is a restructured language used especially for commercial communication). There are legitimate situations for teaching the Bible in a trade language, but it must be done carefully with a redundancy in place to double-check comprehension. Obviously, it is important to correct as much of the language and cultural barrier as possible, but even when one shares the same language, misunderstandings can lead to syncretism.

The subtle danger of syncretistic worship lies in its claim to believe it is worshipping the one true God. Looking back in history, when the Israelites brought idols and idolatrous practices into the Temple, they did not think of their actions as an abandonment of God. They thought of it as just supplementing their worship with customs borrowed from heathen idol worship. Even the golden calf at Mount Sinai was not regarded as a substitute god to replace Yahweh; rather, it was regarded as a symbolic representation of Him. This can be seen in Aaron's reference to the golden calf as the God – *"These are your gods, O Israel, who brought you up out of the land of Egypt!"* – And his proclamation that the worship of the golden calf would be *"...a feast to the Lord"* and not a feast to some Egyptian god (Ex. 32:4b).

Later, Yahweh asked the ancient Israelites a rhetorical question: *"Did ye bring unto me sacrifices and offerings in the wilderness forty years, O house of Israel?"* (Amos 5:25). The answer was, "Yes, they did." They could make a legitimate claim to be following the true God, but there was something more. The next verse explains what they carried in their bags. God said, *"You shall take up Sikkuth your king, and Kiyyun your star-god—your images that you made for yourselves"* (Amos 5:26). These were pagan Assyrian gods. Israel was trying to worship God and idols at the same time.

[THE CHALLENGE OF SYNCRETISM]

A.W. Tozer, former editor of *The Alliance Witness*, once wrote a stimulating editorial entitled, ***Divisions Are Not Always Bad***. He stated:

> When to unite and when to divide is the question. If all unity was good and all division bad then the answer would be simple. If God always united and Satan always divided, the answer would also be easy. But wisdom requires that we divide what should be divided and unite only within God's Word.

The Christian life demands separation from the world and its wisdom, not integration. When writing the letter to the Corinthians, Paul referenced Isaiah 52:11 when he wrote in 2 Cor. 6:17 *"Therefore go out from their midst, and be separate from them, says the Lord, and touch no unclean thing; then I will welcome you."*

The Scriptures reveal syncretism as an ancient tool of Satan to separate God from his people. Nehemiah was faced with syncretic temptation when compromise was offered to him as he rebuilt the wall (Nehemiah 6:2). Church history is filled with the struggle against syncretism from political, social, religious, and economic sources. Relative Syncretism often results from a tendency or attempt to undermine the specific details of the gospel, to make it socially palatable. In our global-village context, secular humanism seems to be the common ground for solving shared social ills; therefore it is carefully woven into the Christian message. The values of this world view strive for a place in the Church's response to the demands for conformity and the cries for liberation.

When missionaries strive for an indigenous national Church with a contextualized gospel, the danger of syncretism is ever present in attempts at accommodation, adjustment, and adaptation. Louis Luzbetak, for instance, wrote in ***The Church and Cultures*** that "there are very few problems plaguing the Missions today that are as serious and as real as the problem of syncretism" (1970, pg. 239). Luzbetak understandably laments the lack of research on syncretism by missionaries and missiologists.

The nature of syncretism makes it difficult to ascertain its extent of influence within a culture. It is not a phenomenon limited to countries where Christianity is more recent. On the contrary, syncretism takes new forms in countries with long-established Christianity. In North America for example, syncretism manifests itself in popular religion such as the current appeal of a gospel of health, wealth and prosperity. We can also detect the phenomenon of religious amalgam in countries where paganism is present. In Asia, the Melanesian Cargo cults located primarily in remote parts of New Guinea offer the most vivid illustration of syncretism. Throughout Melanesia, primitive men await a black Messiah who will bring them a largess of "cargo" (European goods).

In Latin America, the thriving Brazilian spiritism, with millions of adherents, mixes elements of Catholicism with aspects of the religions of the slaves brought from Africa. In the African continent itself, syncretism may be present in the approximately 8,000 African Independent churches which are classified as authentically Christian, but where beliefs and practices are maintained which Christians in other parts of the world might consider pagan.

Many of the traditional figures of popular religious cults in Brazil (often with African roots) are given equivalents from the Christian communion of saints. The result is often the modification and lessening of the challenge from gospel values and from the examples of the Christian saints. Pagan elements predominate over the Christian tradition, even if Christian names are given to such saints and patrons. In Cuba, for example, Yoruba (West African) divinities have been identified with Catholic saints: St. Peter is Elegbara, St. John the Baptist is Ogun.

It is a common saying to describe the religious landscape in Haiti as "90% Catholic and 100% Voodoo." When Roman Catholicism was introduced to the displaced African slaves (in the French colony that is now Haiti), the missionaries made little effort to understand how the Africans viewed

[THE CHALLENGE OF SYNCRETISM]

life and thus did not attempt to clarify the faith, resulting in folk Catholicism and rampant syncretism, which the Roman Catholic Church has been unable to correct to this day. If Protestants do not realize that it is essential to challenge and critique the Haitian's theological presuppositions that help formulate their worldview, then Protestantism in Haiti is destined toward the same end as much of Catholicism in Haiti, a folk religion that is largely devoid of biblical truth.

Missionaries have gravely misinterpreted conversions of many Haitians as a conviction of personal sins and an undefiled acceptance of the Christian faith. While some Haitian believers are properly aligned in the faith, there is a percentage of Haitians who convert for misguided reasons, such as a rebellion against ritual exploitation or domination by the loa (also lwa or l'wha, which are the spirits of Haitian Voodoo), the perception that Protestantism is a superior magical power and the pastor is a more authoritative sorcerer, or as a means by which one can get the *loa* and ancestors to cease meddling in the lives of the new converts. Oftentimes, conversion is related less to a genuine crisis of conscience and more to a pragmatic desire for self-betterment. There are nevertheless many other cultures who mix the biblical message with local traditional religions and superstitions.

Syncretistic Christians can have a dualistic faith perception, which is a problematic aspect of the phenomenon. In the West, this can be seen by the love of recreation, comfort and possessions while simultaneously claiming oneness in Christ within the parameters of acceptable submission. As a result of this inertia, these Christians can find themselves spiritually challenged, unable to progress in the faith vicariously through Christ due to a syncretic alliance with hedonistic pursuits, namely self-fulfillment in the world. The substance of this paradox is quite simple: Christians who are dualistic syncretists can perceive themselves as genuine Christians with little need for heart and life transformation.

A dualistic profession can be convinced inwardly thinking they are in fact on the narrow way, in step with biblical Christianity while in opposition of it. We are given a clear warning in 1 John 2:15 about this deception: *"Do not love the world or the things in the world. If anyone loves the world, the love of the Father is not in him."* Likewise, John's letter of warning written to the Laodicean church in Rev. 3:14-22, addresses similar deception. In the progressive post-modern church, multitudes of confessing Christians have been guided to turn aside from an affinity toward spiritual oneness with God, to find security and identity in worldly fulfillment and success while leaning on the sciences to satisfy reason. If not immediately, they have gradually forsaken the tenants of the faith unaware.

Whatever the case may be, syncretism is a serious challenge to Christian evangelism and missions on a global scale. Surely none of us should "be satisfied with anything less than a Christianity that is in the truest sense of the word an integral part of the local life-way, a twenty-four hour a day affair" (Luzbetak 1970, pg180).

[8]
EVANGELISM AND PHILANTHROPY

In China, India and Pakistan, there have been several generations of humanitarian servitude, brought in by the British missionaries in various forms, starting in the middle of the 18th century. These cultures have watched the English build hospitals, churches and schools for a number of generations. These efforts still progress and regress without any long-term tangible effect on the national Church, the culture served, or society as a whole.

Logically, we should learn from past mistakes in the Church, particularly those in missions and not repeat them. It is typical behavior, to look back and decide that modern missiology has learned a great deal from experience – which we are conducting missions better than previous generations. However, this process of learning from our mistakes is not a straight line of progress. In many ways we still have much to learn from the pioneer leaders in missions, such as William Carey, Henry Venn, John Livingstone, and Hudson Taylor. These are the men who developed the idea of establishing indigenous churches that are self-supporting, self-governing and self-reproducing. Historically speaking, evangelism and philanthropy have been intimately related to one another throughout the history of the Church, although the relationship has been expressed in a variety of ways. Christian missions have often engaged in both activities without biblical clarity, not realizing the ongoing need to carefully define what they were doing or why. Therefore, the problem of their relationship is of particular importance to evangelical Christians.

The Great Awakening in North America, the Pietistic Movement in Germany, and the Evangelical Revival under the Wesley brothers in Britain, which all took place in the early part of the 18th century, initiated a great move toward philanthropy combined with evangelism. The next generation of British evangelicals founded missionary societies and gave conspicuous service in public life. During his parliamentary career, William Wilberforce abolished the slave trade and slavery itself. It was Lord Ashley, Earl of Shaftesbury, who in 1833 heralded the improvement of conditions in the factories, making it illegal for young children to work in textile factories.

However, at the end of the 19th century and the beginning of the 20th, the so-called "Social Gospel" was developed by liberal theologians. Due to worldly thinking, they confused the Kingdom of God with Christian civilization in general, and with social democracy in particular, and they went on to imagine that by their social programs they could build God's kingdom on earth. By contrast, there is the responsible social action which the gospel lays upon us, and the liberal "Social Gospel," which was a perversion of the true gospel once delivered unto the saints.

K. P. Yohannan from his popular book, **Revolution in World Missions**, writes:

> The battle against hunger and poverty is really a spiritual battle, not a physical or social one as secularists would have us believe. The only weapon that will ever effectively win the war against disease, hunger, injustice and poverty in Asia is the gospel of Jesus Christ. To look into the sad eyes of a hungry child or see the wasted life of a drug addict is to see only the evidence of Satan's hold on this world. All bad things, whether in Asia or America, are his handiwork. He is the ultimate enemy of mankind, and he will do everything within his considerable power to kill and destroy human beings. Fighting this powerful enemy with physical weapons is like fighting an armored tank with stones.

Assisting with social needs like daily food, clothing and shelter is the normal outreach of any effective gospel-bearing

[EVANGELISM AND PHILANTHROPY]

ministry. Added to this list could be medical provision and delegation, education, social justice including "abuse activists" and foundations providing refuge from abuse and violence. Additionally, Liberation theology is a modern movement in Christian theology which combines the teachings of Jesus Christ in terms of liberation from unjust economic, political, or social conditions. While these services and positions are good within themselves, they can and do tilt out of balance when a Christian institution collects donations and delegates funding for social needs instead of primarily empowering pastors and planting churches. Social services alone have a tendency to redirect missions away from the primary purpose of Christian missions—evangelism.

Many churches and missions organizations regard social action as a means to evangelism, where by itself it does seem to fulfill the biblical narrative. This ideology promotes the provision of social services as the bait on the hook, while in its best form it gives the gospel an intellectual credibility it would otherwise lack. The enviable results of exploiting and supporting social programs breed what is called "rice Christians," a term used to describe indigenous people of nearly any needy people group or culture who will conform to and adopt the title of any outside entity that will provide for their physical needs. Faced with the choice of starving or converting, many people chose to confess conversion, or to at least appear to convert. This description is very well the inherent flaw in what could be called "felt need" or "symptomatic" aid.

Rice Christian is a literal translation of the Portuguese expression *Christianos de arroz*, which was an insult coined by local non-Christians in Portuguese-influenced areas of East Asia, specifically India and Macao who saw that the poorest and lowest members of society (such as the caste-less people called *pariahs*) were making professions of the Christian faith for the sake of the rice handed out by the missionaries. The Portuguese Roman Catholic missionaries operated in India and Southeast Asia from the early-16th century to the mid-17th century, so the term was likely coined during that period.

In 1931, Mohandas Gandhi wisely noted:

> I hold that proselytizing under the cloak of humanitarian work is, to say the least, unhealthy... Why should I change my religion because a doctor who professes Christianity as his religion has cured me of some disease or why should the doctor expect or suggest such a change whilst I am under his influence? The methods of conversion must be like Caesar's wife above suspicion. Faith is not imparted like secular subjects. It is given through the language of the heart. If a man has a living faith in him, it spreads its aroma like the rose its scent. Because of its invisibility, the extent of its influence is far wider than that of the visible beauty of the colour of the petals.

As servants through Christ in making disciples around the world, we must remember that our task is not simply the dissemination of intellectual information (the plan of salvation) but introducing people to Jesus. This will involve both proclamation (speaking the gospel) and effectual incarnation (living the gospel).

Missionary K.P. Yohannan states that "Social concern is a natural fruit of the gospel. But to put it first is to put the cart before the horse; and from experience, we have seen it fail in India for more than 200 years." Even today, after centuries of proven failure, there are still many missions' organizations and indigenous ministries who concentrate on social services and funding as the core operations while scarcely considering evangelism as the primary purpose. However, the Bible certainly distinguishes between this dichotomy but it also joins them together, and it instructs us to hold the pair in a dynamic and creative tension. It is as wrong to disengage them, as in dualism, as it is to confuse them, as in monism, for they are both part of our Christian duty.

Evangelism does include a degree of social responsibility; we discern the fundamental basis for our actions in the

[Evangelism and Philanthropy]

character of God Himself. He is the God of justice, who in every human community hates evil and loves righteousness. Though God made the universe, He nevertheless humbles Himself to care for the needy, *"executes justice for the oppressed"*, and *"gives food to the hungry"*. In addition: *"The Lord sets the prisoners free; the Lord opens the eyes of the blind. The Lord lifts up those who are bowed down; the Lord loves the righteous. The Lord watches over the sojourners, he upholds the widow and the fatherless; but the way of the wicked he brings to ruin"* (Psalm 146:5-9). He had compassion on the crowds because they were harassed and helpless, like sheep without a shepherd.

When an individual or a small group of Christian believers, who are not properly trained in motive and method of missionary work, creates a para-church outreach ministry, their immediate emotional reaction is to solicit support for their target group, along with supplemental relief provisions and onsite visitation, having only a minimal understanding the evangelism is the most important purpose for missions. James 1:27, Isaiah 1:17 and Matt. 25:36 have become proof texts, banners in which those in provisional alliance march under. When Christians with a heart for missions progress toward maturity in service of God through the Holy Spirit, it will become clear that the Scripture teaches instead to first empower ministries for evangelism and to support evangelists. While social relief is certainly a part of missions, it will always be supplemental to evangelism.

In wanting to affirm that evangelism and social responsibility cooperate with each other, we are not implying that we should refrain from relief operations or that we should view other Christian charities and ministries of compassion as misguided for showing love for those in need. For example, in the case of the Good Samaritan mentioned in Luke 10:29-37, if we may characterize him as a Christian, he could not have been faulted for tending the wounds of the victim and failing to preach to him. Nor is Philip to be blamed for preaching the gospel to the Ethiopian eunuch in his chariot and failing to enquire about his social needs (Acts 8:26-40). There are still occasions when it is legitimate to concentrate on one or the other of these two Christian duties.

It is not erroneous to hold an evangelistic crusade without an accompanying program of social service. Nor is it wrong to feed the hungry in a time of famine before delivering the Good News to them. To quote an African proverb, "an empty belly has no ears." We find a similar situation in the days of Moses. He brought the Israelites in Egypt the good news of their liberation, *"but they did not listen to him, because of their broken spirit and their cruel bondage"* (Exodus 6:9). Nevertheless, with many mission works concentrating on social needs, it is prudent that other missions' organizations become more proactive in the work of evangelism where the Great Commission is presented as a priority.

The best way of relating evangelism and social action is to regard philanthropy not as a means to evangelism but as a manifestation of evangelism. In this case, philanthropy is not attached to evangelism but rather supplemented with the proclamation, proceeding from its natural expression. One might almost say that social action becomes the "sacrament" of evangelism, for it makes the message significantly tangible.

J. Herman Bavinck, in his book ***An Introduction to the Science of Missions***, defends this view. Food, clothing, shelter, medicine and education are more than "a legitimate and necessary means of creating an opportunity for preaching," he writes, for "if these services are motivated by the proper love and compassion, then they cease to be simply preparation, and at that very moment become preaching" (p. 113). Jesus' words and deeds worked together, the words interpreting the deeds and the deeds embodying the words. He did not only announce the good news of the kingdom, but He performed visible "signs of the kingdom." If people would not believe His words, He said, then let them believe Him *"for the sake of the works themselves"* (John 14:11).

[Evangelism and Philanthropy]

Social works will always be a partner of evangelism. As partners, the two belong to each other and yet are independent of each other. There will be times when a person's eternal destiny is the most urgent consideration, for we must not forget that souls without Christ are perishing. But there will be other times when a person's material need is so pressing that they would not be able to hear the gospel if we shared it with them. The man who fell among thieves needed above all else at that moment oil and bandages for his wounds, not a rehearsed evangelism method. A missionary in Nairobi, quoted by Bishop John Taylor, echoes the African proverb of the empty belly by saying that "a hungry man has no ears." If a person is hungry, our biblical mandate is not to evangelize them but to feed them first (Romans 12:20).

Clearly, benevolence and evangelism are interdependent of each other. One might compare evangelism and acts of mercy as the two wings of an airplane. Both are essential, connected to the central purpose, and must not be separated from each other. It is the practice of a word and deed ministry. "Evangelism" is the word portion, and "acts of mercy" are the deed portion, although not distinctly separate. There are times in Scripture when Jesus healed first and then spoke of salvation afterwards, as with the man born blind in John 9 (cf. Mark 5:24b-34). Incidents like this demonstrate that Jesus did not always prioritize spiritual needs over physical needs, since he healed first before calling the man to himself.

This interdependence is further illustrated for us in Matt. 9:2-7 when He first forgave the sins of the paralytic, then healed his body. In John 6:1-13, Jesus miraculously fed 5,000 hungry men, not including women and children in the tally. He performed this miracle after He preached, not before as to give the truth preference. The apostle Peter did not fear to tell the beggar in Acts 3:6, *"I have no silver and gold, but what I do have I give to you. In the name of Jesus Christ of Nazareth, rise up and walk!"* After the miracle, they then preached the gospel of Christ Jesus. However, benevolence never supplants evangelism as the primary purpose of a Christian's ordained commission.

Social provision is a consequence of evangelism, since evangelism is the means by which God brings people to new birth, and their new life manifests itself in the service of others. Paul wrote that *"faith works through love"* (Gal. 5:6), James declared that *"I will show you my faith by my works"* (James 2:18) and John, that God's love within us will overflow in serving our needy brothers and sisters (1 John 3:16-18). Proclaiming Jesus as Lord and Savior (evangelism) has social implications, since it summons people to repent of social as well as personal sins, and to live a new life of righteousness and peace in the new society which challenges the old. Giving food to the hungry (social responsibility) has evangelistic implications, since good works of love, if done in the name of Christ, are a demonstration and commendation of the gospel. Thus, evangelism and social responsibility, while distinct from one another, are integrally related in our proclamation of and obedience to the gospel.

No matter how much assistance we give to the poor, it will never substitute for the saving power and grace of the gospel. Pressing the point again, Jesus did not attempt to eradicate the poverty of his day on a national or aggregate level but instructed his followers to minister to the greatest need of the poor. As Paul says, "For what I received I passed on to you as of first importance: that Christ died for our sins" (1 Cor. 15:3).

[9]
THE PROBLEM OF THE SOCIAL GOSPEL

The "Social Gospel" is an immense challenge for world missions. It is an intellectual movement that was most prominent in the United States and Canada in the early 20th century. While its theories declined after World War I, many of the Social Gospel's ideas reappeared in the Civil Rights Movement of the 1960s. The premise of its principles continues to inspire newer movements today.

The pioneer of the Social Gospel movement was Walter Rauschenbusch, a Baptist who was alarmed by the plight of the poor in places ranging from the New York Bronx to the working class neighborhoods of Chicago's South Side. Rauschenbusch and other Social Gospel advocates wanted to make Christianity relevant to the social crisis in areas including liquor traffic to housing conditions to labor negotiations to global peacemaking. But the Social Gospel advocates weren't simply "applying" historic orthodox Christianity to these problems. The seeming impotence of traditional Christianity to address these issues was, for the Social Gospel pioneers, evidence that something was wrong with Christianity as an institution.

Rauschenbusch's view of Christianity was that its purpose was to enlarge the Kingdom of God, not by preaching the torments of hell or other fear-inducing messages, but by leading a Christ-like life by acts of kindness. The belief was, and is, that Christianity will attract followers when it demonstrates its love for mankind. This could be best accomplished by helping to alleviate the suffering of humanity caused by poverty, disease, oppressive work conditions, society's injustices, civil rights abuses, etc. Those who fostered this movement also believed that relief from their conditions of misery would improve the moral nature of those so deprived.

Rauschenbusch did not view Jesus' death as an act of substitutionary atonement but in his book ***A Theology for the Social Gospel*** he states that Jesus died "...to substitute love for selfishness as the basis of human society." He wrote that "Christianity is in its nature revolutionary" and tried to remind society of this premise. He explained that the Kingdom of God "is not a matter of getting individuals to heaven, but of transforming the life on earth into the harmony of heaven." Because of his views, Rauschenbusch ideologies were largely condemned as heretical.

Traditional Protestant thought held that the salvation of the individual would lead to social improvement, and so social improvement was never considered an end in itself. Certainly a just society would make the job of the Church easier, but it could only be achieved by converting one individual at a time. Adherents came to believe that individuals could only depart from sinful lifestyles and habits if they were removed from the social and economic situations that had driven them into sin in the first place.

As a result of this reasoning, individual salvation was important, but considered secondary to social reform, which would convert multitudes into God's kingdom as the government and economic institutions themselves taught men and women of brotherly love. Salvation of the individual, then, stood as an important byproduct of working for a literal Kingdom of God on earth. Working for social improvement, the Kingdom of God on earth, then, was the thrust of the Social Gospel movement.

Progressive-minded preachers began to tie the teachings of the church with contemporary problems. Christian virtue, they declared, demanded a redress of poverty and despair on earth. Many ministers became politically active in this reform. Washington Gladden, a leading member of the Progressive Movement, was the most prominent of the

[THE PROBLEM OF THE SOCIAL GOSPEL]

social gospel ministers. He supported the workers' right to strike in the wake of the Great Upheaval of 1877. Ministers aggressively called for an end to child labor, the enactment of temperance laws, and civil service reform.

Liberal churches such as the Congregationalists and the Unitarians led the way, but the movement spread throughout many denominational sects. Middle class women became particularly active in the arena of social reform. The Young Men's Christian Association and the Young Women's Christian Association were formed to address the problems of urban youth. The Social Gospel principles continued to inspire movements such as Christians Against Poverty.

Theologically, the Social Gospel leaders were overwhelmingly post-millennialist, meaning they believed the Second Coming could not happen until humankind rid itself of social evils by human effort. For the most part, they rejected pre-millennialist theology, according to which the Second Coming of Christ was imminent, and Christians should devote their energies to prepare for Christ's soon return rather than addressing the issue of social evils. Their millennial views are very similar to those shared by modern Christian Reconstructionists.

The Social Gospel, in all of its assorted applications, helped to produce some achievements that have contributed to the welfare of society, such as abolishing child labor and regulating long hours worked by mothers. It became the primary gospel of liberal liberal and progressive theologians and mainline denominations throughout the 20th century. Although its popularity alternately rose and fell as it ran its course, it was often energized by the combination of religion and liberal politics, for example Martin Luther King Jr. and the civil rights movement. In the midst of the last century and later, the Social Gospel influenced developments such as the liberation theology of Roman Catholicism and the socialism of left-leaning evangelical Christians. It is in this present century, however, that the Social Gospel has received its most extensive promotion, advanced within the Church.

We often hold highest the humanistic ideals of happiness, freedom and economic, cultural and social progress for all mankind. This secular teaching declares, "Since all men are brothers," we should work for that which contributes toward the welfare of all men. The worldview will not point to sin as the root cause of all human suffering. The current emphasis of modern evangelism is that we should holistically operate missions that provide "care for the whole man," but it instead ends up providing help for only the body — often ignoring the direst need of the soul, a spiritual rebirth.

The Social Gospel did indeed advocate evangelism, but the evangelism was often a means to an end, to the "Christianization" of a locality or of the world so that social change might result. Because progressives of this age often believed Christianity was the evolutionary pinnacle of human religion, they believed a modern Christian identity could democratize, and thus civilize, the heathen social barbarisms around the world. Christian missions then would mean improved lifestyles, more just industrial policies, better living conditions for women and children, and so forth.

This teaching has prospered within the Church and has taken on many different forms. It not only has corrupted the motives and framework of missions, but has altered local ministry as well, creating a man-centered gospel based on changing the external perception and the social status of a person, through meeting their physical and emotional needs. This contamination of missions has a tendency to subdue or sometimes remove God's divine redemption found in the gospel message.

Because of this teaching, many churches and missionary societies are redirecting their limited outreach funds and personnel away from evangelism to something that can be called "social concerns." A number of Christian missionaries find themselves primarily involved in feeding the hungry,

[THE PROBLEM OF THE SOCIAL GOSPEL]

caring for the sick, assisting with education, housing the homeless or other kinds of relief and development work. As mentioned previously, while these may be a part of missions, social support alone is not the biblical model of evangelism. This reflects the separationist's view between humanitarian philanthropy and consideration of those in spiritual and physical destitution.

In the Abrahamic faiths, especially Christianity, care for the poor is an overarching fruit or "proof of action" of a transitioned spirit, from darkness to light. If one truly has encountered God's Spirit and the heart is changed, the new inclination is no longer to seek only self and one's own sphere of family alone, but the heart extends to all those who are in need, in as much as is possible. For example, from Wisdom of Solomon, which many civilizations revere, related passages read *"When you help the poor you are lending to the Lord--and he pays wonderful interest on your loan!"* (Proverbs 19:17) and *"Anyone who oppresses the poor is insulting God who made them. To help the poor is to honor God."* (Proverbs 14:31) and *"If you give to the poor, your needs will be supplied! But a curse upon those who close their eyes to poverty"* (Proverbs 28:27).

While this "spirit of outreach" for the destitute should not be purposely dedicated for social considerations alone, such as erecting buildings, developing schools, establishing medical stations, and creating sewing centers as examples, where the meeting of physical and social needs are not the essential tenets of evangelism, but may still be a part of evangelism in context to biblical Christianity. However, this is an area where donation misallocations occur in many mission programs. Recipient organizations sometimes unwittingly misuse donations, redistributing funds and resources without comprehension of the true purpose of missions, which is first and foremost evangelism.

Perhaps the best way to understand our responsibilities in the social/cultural arena is to look to Jesus for our example.

Jesus perfectly maintained His Father's perspective on social and political matters, even though He lived in a society that was every bit as pagan and corrupt as today's culture. Cruel tyrants and dictators ruled throughout the region, and the institution of slavery was firmly entrenched. Legal and economic oppression of the Jews by Rome was rampant, dwarfing anything we experience today. But even in the face of such tyranny, Jesus never issued a call for political changes, even by peaceful means. He never attempted to "capture the culture" for biblical morality. He did not come to earth to be a political or social reformer. Rather, He came to establish a new spiritual order founded on an atoning sacrifice—Himself. He came not to make the old order moral through social and governmental reform, but to make His new creatures holy through the saving power of the gospel and the transforming work of the Holy Spirit.

Ultimately, the Social Gospel of the early twentieth century was in large ineffective spiritually and physically, nor will this outcome change regardless of any redefinition of it. Without that which makes Christianity's "scandal of the cross" unique, people will keep the social program but substitute a religion, whether secular or pagan, that better allows them to "*continue in sin that grace may abound*" (Rom. 6:1). This is why the groups that embraced the Social Gospel during last century are now contaminated shells of previous Christian convictions. The Social Gospels of yesterday and today are correct in noting that an isolationist, a separatist Christianity fails to acknowledge the wholeness found in Christ through salvation. They are misled, though, in the removal of personal sin, personal redemption, and personal reconciliation as the way to redeem a Christian identity.

As we have studied and concluded, a person's physical needs have nothing to do with their heart's condition of being in rebellion against a holy God. An unregenerate rich man in London or a poor lost beggar in Bombay are both rebels against God, according to the Scripture. For all humankind,

[THE PROBLEM OF THE SOCIAL GOSPEL]

the only way to become a child of God and inherit His promise of eternal life is to repent and accept Jesus Christ as Savior. The evident fruit of Satan's scheme is that during the last hundred years, the focus has shifted away from the pure, simple proclamation of this message to investing efforts and funding into social work.

Providing bags of rice or shelter will never save a soul and will rarely change the condition of a person's heart. Yes, the recipient will be very grateful, but their hearts cannot be changed without the power of God's transforming Spirit through Jesus Christ. *"No one can come to me unless the Father who sent me draws him"* (John 6:44). In John 6:26, we read that Jesus rebuked the multitude because He knew their hearts, *"I tell you the truth; you are looking for me, not because you saw miraculous signs but because you ate the loaves and had your fill."* A multitude followed him because they thought they had found a source of free food but then departed when they realized their physical needs were not going to be met. The crowds recognized the miracles of Christ, and concluded he must be a prophet; but they had a greater concern for their own worldly interest, and their earthly appetites, than the life-giving words that Jesus offered. Even today, many are those who make a profession of their faith in Christ, but their primary ambition is worldly gain and physical pleasures, not the spiritual and everlasting.

Any gospel that removes the cross of judgment against sin, that separates the gospel from personal reconciliation with God and with others, is not the gospel of Jesus Christ. Likewise, any type of Christianity that turns us away from the divine revelations about Jesus—his deity, his humanity, virgin birth, his suffering on the cross, his bodily resurrection, his future return, his authority in Scripture, his building of the Church—is pointing us to some different Messiah. The good news is social but the Social Gospel isn't good news.

The core problem with the Social Gospel, even when it is clothed in religious garments and operating within Christian institutions, is that it seeks to defeat what is basically a spiritual warfare with weapons of the flesh. As the apostle Paul wrote in 2 Cor. 10:4, *"For the weapons of our warfare are not of the flesh, but mighty before God to the casting down of strong holds."* Indeed, our battle is not against flesh and blood or the darkness that bears fruits like poverty and hunger. It is against Satan and his countless demons who toil day and night to drag human souls into a Christ-less eternity.

When God's Spirit touches and changes the heart of a man or woman, the physical experience for that person will change as well. This inner change may not regenerate a new limb or remove a life threatening illness, although it could. The point is if one continues in a life indwelt with the Spirit of God, a person's choices will change, resulting in a constantly revised physical life and experience. If we want to help meet the needs of the poor and starving in this world, there is no better place to start than by sharing the gospel of salvation which can change the cold heart into a fountain of life. The regenerative work of God will do more to lift up the downtrodden, the hungry and the needy than all the social programs meticulously developed by humanists.

Ours is a spiritual battle against worldly ideologies and dogmas that are arrayed against God's revealed counsel, and we achieve victory over them only with the weapons of biblical revelation (2 Cor. 10:3-5). The Bible declares all the man-made philosophies and religions of the world to be "illegitimate" and "consigned" not to "some kind of evil end" but to their just end. Only belief in the biblical gospel saves humanity.

[10]
THE ENEMY VERSUS THE POWER OF GOD

As Christians, we have learned that the Bible teaches that there are essentially two opposing powers at conflict. There is the worship of the one monotheistic God in truth and reverence, and then there is a false demonic religious system that appears in many forms, and holds dominion in the World. However, God and Satan are not two equal powers in a dualistic battle between good and evil, as the theology of dualism summates. A common representation of these opposites is known from the Taoist religion as Yin and Yang. Dualism is unbiblical since Scripture does not teach that the universe consists of opposites, nor does it affirm that Satan and God are equal and opposing forces. God, according to Scripture, is infinitely greater than Satan and will eventually cast Satan into hell. Our Lord reigns as the supreme Creator and King of the universe. His sovereign will is being accomplished in the universe and spiritual realm whether or not His creation accepts Him as Lord.

Throughout the history of mankind, evil has always sought to enslave, discriminate and divide. In Asia for example, there is a faith system invented in ancient Persia. Between 1500-800 BCE, the Persians and the Medes, two groups of Aryan nomads, migrated to the Iranian plateau from central Asia. Most historians believe that the Aryans invaded India and caused the collapse of the Indus Civilization circa 1500 BCE, having poured over the Hindu Kush Mountains. The Aryans' (Indo-Persians) armies and priests spread their faith to India where it took root. Hindu missionaries in turn spread it throughout the rest of Asia. Animism, Jainism, Buddhism and all other Asian religions have a common heritage in this mystical religious system.

[Finding the Balance in World Missions]

With the advent of the Christian missionaries in India under the patronage of the British rule in the 18th century, a new chapter of proselytization began. These missionaries concentrated their charity work mainly in the tribal areas, telling the people that they were not Hindus, that their indigenous culture and religion was different from Hinduism. The missionaries were able to use the leverage of history to convert those who were most affected by caste prejudice. They taught them that Christianity, an alien religion, was their own, that Jesus Christ who was born and lived in the Middle-East was also a 'Dalit' like them and that Christianity was a religion without the caste bias and offered them socio-economic equality. In their desire to lead a life of respect, thousands of tribal people were converted to Christianity under the assumption that they had found an answer to the wretched caste system lodged in Hinduism.

Little did they know that conversion to Christianity would not redeem them from social discrimination and from being 'untouchables', because though Jesus never advocated the caste system, Christianity in India was not free from the caste bias. Christian missionaries criticized Hinduism for its caste system whilst upholding discrimination based on a caste system within their churches. In spite of the fact that around 75% of the Christians are 'Dalits' who were converted to Christianity to dispose of their 'outcaste' designation, Dalit Christians within the church were discriminated against and were denied powers within the ecclesiastical structure.

Even today, the caste system among Indian Christians often reflects stratification by sect (Sikhs, Jainas, etc.), location, and the castes of their predecessors. In Kerala for example, the Syrian Christians or Nasranis did not cooperate with the evangelical activities of foreign missionaries in allowing new converts to join their community since they were afraid that their noble position in the society could have been endangered. Social practices among some Indian Christians parallel much of the discrimination faced by lower castes in other religious communities, as well as having attributes unique to this community. Social inertia caused old traditions and biases against other castes to remain, resulting in caste segregation that persists among Indian Christians. About 70–80% of Indian Christians are members of the Dalit or backward classes.

In Goa, despite the presence of Portuguese missionaries from the 16th century, the Hindu converts retained their caste practices. Thus, the original Hindu Brahmins in Goa became Christian *Bamonns* and the Kshatriya and Vaishya Vanis became Christian noblemen called *Chardos*. In Tamil Nadu, Indian Christian Dalits also complain of discrimination by the Telugu-speaking Reddiar minority. Indian law does not provide benefits for Dalit Christians; however Christians have been striving for the same rights given to Hindu, Buddhist, and Sikh Scheduled castes. Caste discrimination is strongest among Christians in South India and weaker among urban Protestant congregations in North India. This is due to the fact that in South India, whole castes converted en masse to the faith, leaving members of different castes to compete in ways parallel to Hindus of the Indian caste system. One of the most complex systems of segregation, and what later became a system of discrimination, has been that of caste in India.

The agony we see in the faces of the starving children and beggars in photos and on television is a culmination of centuries of religious slavery to occult practices, godless systems like the caste discriminations and the bondage to sin. Additionally, poverty in today's global village has become the growing cause of evil among mankind, because it has power and the ability to make people compromise their once held and respected moral values, cultures and religious beliefs.

The fact that evil exists throughout our world seems incontrovertible. We see evil every day in its infernally multifarious forms. First, there are the cosmic, supernatural, transpersonal, or natural evils like floods, famine, fire, drought, disease, earthquakes, tornadoes, hurricanes, and harmful, unforeseeable accidents that wreak untimely death, havoc, and unmentionable suffering on humanity. Such examples are metaphysical or existential evils with which the biblical Book of Job concerns itself, and which religions worldwide try with great effort to explain. Existential evil is an inescapable part of our human destiny, and one with which we must reckon as best we can, without closing ourselves off to its tragic, intrinsic reality. But there is, of course, another kind of evil at large: human evil, mankind's inhumanity to mankind in the most panoramic sense. By human evil, we mean those attitudes and behaviors that promote excessive interpersonal aggression, cruelty, hostility, disregard for the integrity of others, self-destructiveness, psychopathology and human misery in general. Human evil can be perpetrated by a single individual (personal evil) or by a group, a country, or an entire culture (collective evil).

Asia makes up the vast majority of the 3.8 billion (2012 census) overlooked people who are being missed by traditional missionary efforts and evangelism budgets. This missionary zone is inhabited by those who are spiritually bound by strongholds, ignorantly trapped in an ancient satanic spiritual system. One of the factors in understanding India's hunger and poverty problem is the Hindu belief system and its effect on food production. Most people know about the sacred cow as an idiom, a figurative reference to revered cows that roam the streets, freely eating quality grain while local people starve. Centuries ago, the cow was designated as the appropriate gift to the Brahmans (highest-caste priests) and it was soon said that to kill a cow is equal to killing a Brahman. The importance of the pastoral element in the Krishna stories, particularly from the 10th century onward, further reinforced the sanctity of the cow. However, a lesser-known and more sinister culprit is another animal protected by religious belief, the common rat.

| The Enemy Versus the Power of God |

Reincarnation is believed to be the transmigration of the soul from one life form to another. It doesn't just apply to humans but to all creatures and some non-living things as well. If a person has lived an unworthy life he or she moves down the scale, say, from a lower caste to a rat. Therefore, the rat must be protected as a likely recipient of a reincarnated soul on its way up the ladder of spiritual evolution to ascend to nirvana. Though many in India reject this and seek to rid their homes of rats, large-scale efforts at extermination have been impeded by religious resistance.

The following is an excerpt from an article in the *India Express*:

> Dashnok is a small village near Nokha in Bikaner district, location of the famous Karni Mata temple. Hundreds of brown rats, called 'Kabas' by the devotees, scurry around merrily in the large compound of the temple and sometimes even around the image of the goddess. The rats are fed on prasad offered by the devotee or by the temple management, whereas these rats are believed to house the souls of Karni Mata's departed devotees.
>
> One has to walk cautiously through the temple compound; for if a rat is crushed to death, it is not only considered a bad omen but may also invite severe punishment. One is considered lucky if a rat climbs over one's shoulder. Better still to see a white rat. People from all over India pay a holy visit to Shri karni Mata temple during Navratri.

In many Asian villages, traditional religions still have a powerful hold on the minds of the inhabitants. Almost every village or community has a preferred idol or deity—there are 330 million gods, goddesses, or demigods in the Hindu pantheon alone. In addition, various animistic cults, which involve the worship of demon spirits, are openly practiced alongside Islam, Hinduism and Buddhism. In many locations, the village temple remains the center of informal education, tourism and civic pride. Religion is big business, and temples take in vast sums of money annually. Millions of priests and amateur practitioners of the occult arts also are profiting from the continuation and expansion of traditional area religions.

Despite all the large-scale social programs provided by the Church and secular world organizations, the problem of hunger and poverty continues to grow in various countries. The real culprit is not a person, lack of natural resources or a system of government. It is about souls bound in spiritual darkness. This satanic stronghold thwarts every effort to make progress using humanistic wisdom and programs. It enslaves the Asian people and those in other countries with similar bondage, to misery in this world and its deceptions. The single most important social reform that can be brought to the world is the gospel of Jesus Christ. According to the Joshua Project (as of February 2013) there are 16,594 people groups in the world. 7,162 of these are "unreached" (fewer than 2% evangelical). The number arrived at was 2.87 billion people living today who have never heard the Gospel. Of these, 1 billion people in India and Pakistan alone have never heard the name of Jesus Christ. These cultures and many other locations in the world need the hope and truth that only the Lord Jesus Christ can provide.

[11]
GOOD INTENTIONS WITHOUT GUIDANCE

If we've heard it once, we've heard it a thousand times: "Those who ignore history are destined to repeat it." Indeed, we can't correct the mistakes of the past unless we know what they are, and understand their negative impact on our lives. In this category, Christianity seems to have a colossal case of nearsightedness regarding its mission into the world. In short, our desire to put people under the hearing of the Gospel drives us to create missions strategies that reach around the globe, but at the same time we tend to bypass our responsibility "to contend for the faith" (Jude 3) in the midst of our own culture. This has happened in the past, and with catastrophic results. Unless Christians contend for the faith within our own culture, we'll lose the culture, and even become corrupted ourselves.

Because of doctrinal "refining" on the non-essentials, a desire to be comfortable, and increase in apathy, churches found among affluent nations, in many respects, have become weakened. The pursuit of comfort and "doctrinal purity" has robbed the Church of much of its intended power. Where the early Christians had to rely on God for their every need, today creature-comforts and consumerist churches have made many of us complacent and sluggish to the call of God to make disciples of every nation. Wealthy nations only need to put on credit what their whims demand and thereby avoid the dependence upon God for daily needs; this makes faith in God less pressing. Many Christians have become distracted and the Church is showing signs of spiritual apathy as Christian humanism evolve unabated.

Humanism itself was a real historical movement, but it was never a philosophy or a religion. It belongs to the sphere of education, not to that of theology or metaphysics. No doubt it involved certain moral values, but so does any educational tradition. Christian humanism has its roots in the traditional teaching that humans are made in the image of God, which is the basis of individual worth and personal dignity. Christian humanism emphasizes the humanity of Jesus, his social teachings and his predisposition to synthesize human spirituality and materialism. It regards humanist principles like universal human dignity and individual freedom and the primacy of human happiness as essential and principal components of, or at least compatible with, the teachings of Jesus. Since the advent of postmodernism, some radical, "progressive" Christians have choose to view the Christ of faith as irreconcilable with the Jesus of history, regarding the latter as a distinctly fallible mortal. Christian humanism has change shape many times throughout history, gravely affecting missions in its wake.

K.P. Yohannan discusses candidly from his book ***Revolution in World Missions***, about the misgivings of misallocated efforts in missions:

> I first learned this horrible truth about the ineffectiveness of humanitarian aid in the late 1970s at a North India survey expedition before we first went to preach. Throughout the Indian churches, the various mission hospitals and schools of North India are well-known. My coworkers and I eagerly looked forward to visiting some of these missionaries and seeing the local churches. We especially wanted to meet the believers in the villages near these famed mission stations. To our amazement we could not find a living congregation anywhere. There were hardly any believers at all. The surrounding villages were as deep in spiritual darkness as they had been two hundred years ago before the missionaries came. We were shocked to find after eighty to one hundred years of constant mission work, and after an investment of millions of dollars in these areas, few churches existed. As I have traveled throughout India and many other Asian nations, I have seen this same scenario repeated over and over.

[Good Intentions Without Guidance]

In few countries is the failure of Christian humanism more apparent than in Thailand. The Portuguese were the first Europeans to arrive in Thailand in 1518 and they were allowed to open a Christian mission. In fact, the Thai king gave a large donation to build the first Christian (Roman Catholic) Church in the country. Under King Narai, who was interested in the West, European missionaries and adventurers exerted considerable influence in the royal court. However, when King Narai died in 1688, members of the government, fearing the missionaries' proselytizing efforts, killed or expelled all Westerners from Thailand. It remained a closed country to Europeans for the next 100 years.

In 1780, King Taksin allowed French missionaries to enter Thailand, and like the previous Thai king, helped them build a church. In the early 19th century it was estimated that there were 1,000 Thai Christians in Bangkok, descendants of the Portuguese who were widely intermarried with the Thais. Protestant missionaries arrived in 1828, and the continuous residence of American missionaries dates from 1833 to the present day. After 18 years, 22 missionaries had failed to make one convert, but their non-religious efforts had a profound social impact. They had brought modern knowledge and western medicine to the country. For example, in 1835, American missionaries set up the first printing press using the Thai alphabet.

Well-intentioned missionaries probably have done more to modernize Thailand than any other single world entity. They gave the country the core of its civil service, education and medical systems. Working closely with the royal family, the missionaries played a crucial role in eliminating slavery and keeping the country free of western control during the colonial era.

Today, virtually all that remains of this is a shell of Christian good works, where over 95% of the Thai people are currently devotees of the Theravada Buddhist sect. Millions of Thai of the social and economic growth period, who never heard the gospel, have meanwhile slipped into Christ-less eternity without knowing Jesus. They died more educated, better governed and healthier thanks to the good intentions of Christian mission programs, but they died without Christ and are eternally separated from the Creator.

What went wrong? Were these missionaries not dedicated enough? Were their doctrines unscriptural? Perhaps they did not believe in eternal hell or eternal heaven. Did they lack proper Scripture training, or did they simply fail to share the good news? Maybe they shifted their priorities from being interested in saving souls to relieving human suffering? In honesty, collected accounts indicate it was probably a combination of all of these issues. After hundreds of years of showing social compassion, Christianity still makes up only one-tenth of one percent of the entire Thai population.

We must also consider the mistake of the humanists of the Renaissance and the men of the eighteenth century, and to some extent of modern scholars, is that they have regarded the humanist tradition as the only creative and formative element in the Western culture. They have shut their eyes to the existence of another tradition which is even more important than humanism—the Christian faith. The Christian faith and missions unfortunately, like the tradition of humanism, has become acclimatized and assimilated after many years of human refinements.

It is true that Christianity is not bound up with any particular race or culture. It is neither of the East nor of the West, but has a universal mission to the human race as a whole. Nevertheless it is precisely in this universality that the natural bond and affinity between Christianity and humanism is to be found. Humanism is an attempt to overcome the curse of Babel which divides mankind into a mass of warring tribes pitted against one another by their mutual incompatibility.

It becomes apparent that there can be no suitable alliance between Christianity and Humanism, or rather the de facto

[GOOD INTENTIONS WITHOUT GUIDANCE]

alliance that does in some sort exist is a compromising one from which Christians must disentangle themselves. However, after 1800 years of cohesive agreement, there has been so much mutual acceptance that all kinds of patterns of thought and behavior have been formed which has become second nature to the Church. The average Christian does not realize how much his or her moral and social obligation is conditioned by humanist influences.

K.P. Yohannan reflects upon the fruitful missionaries:

> I met poor, often minimally educated, native brothers involved in gospel work in pioneer areas. They had nothing material to offer the people to whom they preached—no agricultural training and no medical relief or school program. But hundreds of souls were saved, and in a few years, a number of churches were established. What were these brothers doing right to achieve such results, while the others with many more advantages had failed?
>
> The answer lies in our basic understanding of what mission work is all about. There is nothing wrong with charitable acts—but they are not to be confused with preaching the gospel. Feeding programs can save a man dying from hunger. Medical aid can prolong life and fight disease. Housing projects can make this temporary life more comfortable—but only the gospel of Jesus Christ can save a soul from a life of sin and an eternity in hell!

In the book ***A Chance to Die*** by Elizabeth Elliot, she quotes renowned missionary Amy Carmichael who stated,

> The devil does not care how many hospitals we build, any more than he cares how many schools and colleges we put up, if only he can pull our ideals down, and sidetrack us on to anything of any sort except the living of holy, loving, humble lives, and the bringing of men, women and children to know our Lord Jesus Christ not only as Savior but as Sovereign Lord.

One of the reasons that these errors can continue is the Church has too many missionaries, pastors, and evangelists who don't understand biblical conversion–a grave problem which has resulted in the utter destruction of souls all around the world as missionaries go forth and win converts to their methodologies, traditions, or denomination rather than winning souls to Christ.

We must understand that conversion is a supernatural miracle of God, that salvation is of the Lord, that regeneration is absolutely essential to genuine conversion, and that a real convert will bear evidence through a new life in Christ. Genuine conversion results in a life of practical obedience to the commandments of Jesus Christ under the New Covenant in a growing holiness and love for the Lord. No soul has been converted who lives a lifestyle of continual immorality and ungodliness. Everyone who is born of God will not continue in the practice of sin (1 John 3:3-9).

It should be a firm conviction that there is only one manner of biblical conversion; only one proper response to the gospel and that is through repentance and faith. While salvation is by grace alone apart from works, the fact remains that those who truly receive God's grace will respond to it by turning from sin and devoting their life to the Lord Jesus Christ.

[12]
PERSUADED TO SHARE CHRIST

When a Christian is filled with the love of God, they cannot help but submit to the Spirit's persuasion to get involved in some form of outreach ministry. It is a natural overflow of God's Spirit dwelling within them. If we do not have any yearning for the lost or the suffering, but instead covet resources of time and possessions for self, immediate family and frivolous pleasures, then we are such as those who may either not know Jesus or in disobedience choose to ignore our call to love others as ourselves. As is stated in 1 John 4:20, *"If anyone says, "I love God," and does not care for his brother, he is a liar; for he who does not love his brother whom he has seen cannot love God whom he has not seen."*

If the Lord revealed to us God's own heart and His statutes, He will teach us compassion for those who reject Him. This was the mind of Jesus. His life exhibited one, whose "heart was made of tenderness." A genuine Christian will be conformed to the image of his Lord. His heart will therefore be touched with a tender concern for the honor of his God, and deeply moved with concern for the sinners that keep not his law, who are perishing in their transgressions.

As did Moses *"Then I lay prostrate before the LORD as before, forty days and forty nights. I neither ate bread nor drank water, because of all the sin that you had committed, in doing what was evil in the sight of the LORD to provoke him to anger"* (Deut. 9:18). Thus also Samuel, in the anticipation of the Lord's judgments upon Saul, *"and he cried out to the LORD all that night"* (1 Sam. 15:11, 35). So does Ezra, on a similar occasion, in the deepest prostration of sorrow, *"I tore my tunic and cloak, pulled hair from my head and beard and sat down appalled"* (Ezra 9:3).

Do we hear the call to *"Let the priests, the LORD'S ministers, Weep between the porch and the altar"* (Joel 2:17a NASB)? How instructive is the attitude of the prophet of old—first pleading openly with the rebellion of the people—then *"I will weep in secret because of your pride; my eyes will weep bitterly, overflowing with tears..."* (Jer. 13:17). Nor was He any less instructive as the apostle—his *"I am speaking the truth in Christ—I am not lying; my conscience bears me witness in the Holy Spirit—that I have great sorrow and unceasing anguish in my heart"* (Rom. 9:1-2). In reproving the rebellious, he could only write to them, *"Out of much affliction and anguish of heart with many tears"* (2 Cor. 2:4), and in speaking of them to others, with the same tenderness of spirit, he adds: *"Of whom I tell you even weeping"* (Phil. 3:18; Comp. Acts 20:19). There were tears of Christians who spoke or wrote with eloquence but with nothing less than with Christian compassion.

As pointed out in previous chapters, the post-modern church places a great deal of emphasis on humanitarian outreach by meeting the physical needs of the needy. However, it is not enough to help the needy alone as an expression of biblical outreach. In comparison, even the humanitarian atheist is moved with compassion about social concerns. Count the number of foundations created by the Hollywood elite who have no preference of faith, but donate millions to humanitarian causes. With nearly the same motives, we also have countless churches involved in short-term missionary campaigns, enlisting large numbers who embark on a missionary journey, but resume life as usual when they return home. The fruit of the pseudo-Christian humanitarian is in stride with the Social Gospel, which places an emphasis on the temporal and the physical while realizing only a marginal comprehension of the eternal coupled with spiritually awakened Holy Spirit compassion.

Among Christians by profession, it is said that 95% are not personally involved in evangelism or the Great Commission.

[PERSUADED TO SHARE CHRIST]

This means that only the remaining 5% of the church actively shares their faith (which includes pastoral staff), while the vast majority remain seated on the sidelines. Why then is sharing our faith such a problem for the church if what we believe is the answer for eternal redemption and the many sociological, political, and world problems?

First, some argue that the Great Commission was only given to the apostles and therefore does not apply to us today. While it is true that contextually the Great Commission (Matt. 28:18-20) was given to the apostles, it was not only for the apostles. The command *"teaching them to observe all that I have commanded you"* certainly includes the charge to make disciples, which included not only the apostles but also every believer in Christ.

Second, some claim that since only a select number of people has the "gift of evangelism," not everyone is obligated to witness. Space prohibits a detailed discussion on the topic of "the gift of evangelism," but a few observations are in order. In the first place, evangelism for one is not recorded in the common spiritual gifts listings in Scripture; instead, the office of evangelist is mentioned in Eph. 4:11. Some theologians rightly question whether "evangelism" should be labeled as a distinct spiritual gift, such as giving, serving, and the others listed in Scripture. However, even if evangelism is a spiritual gift, it is also a command for all believers, as are the service gifts. If a believer decides that he or she does not have "the gift of evangelism" is not an excuse from his or her call to share Christ with others.

Another reason many professing Christians lack any internal persuasion towards evangelism is unbelief about aspects of the faith, which could mean they are not genuinely in Christ and thus cannot adhere to the teachings of God-inspired Scripture. We know it is impossible to please God without faith, *"And without faith it is impossible to please him, for whoever would draw near to God must believe that he exists and that he rewards those who seek him"*

(Heb. 11:6). Also, the righteous must live by faith, *"but my righteous one shall live by faith, and if he shrinks back, my soul has no pleasure in him"* (Heb. 10:38). Many are they who have not yet entered into salvation, even among those who have maintained regular church attendance for 20-50 years, laity and clergy, who are still dead in their sins.

A soul bound by sin or worldly preoccupation will only with great effort, ever consider any evangelism-missionary work or support of it. Once our heart is transformed and made positionally right with God through Christ Jesus, we will be motivated beyond restraint to share the gospel, to get involved in the work of harvesting souls. Do not mistake the motivation of works justification, being active for the sake of righteous appearance, or to satisfy the feelings of obligation. We should not be deceived, for any number of base ambitions can motivate fleshly activities in evangelism, without empowerment from the Holy Spirit. All of us must carefully examine our motives. The Psalmists reflects this in Psalms 26:2: *"Prove [test] me, O Lord, and try me; test my heart and my mind."*

Paul exhorted the Corinthians with a sobering inquiry: *"Examine yourselves to see whether you are in the faith; test yourselves. Do you not realize that Christ Jesus is in you--unless, of course, you fail the test?"* (2 Cor. 13:5). We know that the particular reason why Paul calls on them to examine themselves was that there was occasion to fear that many of them had been deceived. The examination asks whether we are true Christians, whether we have any true faith in the gospel message. Faith in Jesus Christ, and in the promises of God through Him, is one of the distinguishing characteristics of a true Christian, and the ascertaining of true faith is to discover whether we are sincere Christians. Our fruit is our living testimony and declaration, for we read in Scripture: *"But what comes out of the mouth proceeds from the heart"* (Matt. 15:18).

[Persuaded to Share Christ]

St. Clement, Bishop of Rome (100 AD) who was purportedly consecrated by Saint Peter, and whose letters were read in churches, along with other epistles, described this historical truth in his letter to the Corinthians, chapter 42:

> The Apostles preached to us the Gospel received from Jesus Christ, and Jesus Christ was God's Ambassador. Christ, in other words, comes with a message from God, and the Apostles with a message from Christ. Both these orderly arrangements, therefore, originate from the will of God. And so, after receiving their instructions and being fully assured through the Resurrection of our Lord Jesus Christ, as well as confirmed in faith by the word of God, they went forth, equipped with the fullness of the Holy Spirit, to preach the good news that the Kingdom of God was close at hand. From land to land, accordingly, and from city to city they preached; and from among their earliest converts appointed men whom they had tested by the Spirit to act as bishops and deacons for the future believers.

The moment we are saved, we become ambassadors for Christ. The Holy Spirit gives us boldness and the power to share with conviction. No specific training is required to share our testimony; the testimony of our salvation is where it starts. Messiah Missions aids Asian Christians who live in Hindu or Muslim communities, where they have been beaten and homes burnt for the name of Christ. Their life is a living profession despite daily peril. At the same time, many in the modern church carefully protect their self-esteems from offense and offending others by claiming their faith as a private matter, not willing to share the gospel. Jesus clearly shares God's heart about this in Luke 9:26: *"For whoever is ashamed of Me and My words, the Son of Man will be ashamed of him when He comes in His glory, and the glory of the Father and of the holy angels."*

To proclaim the good news about the salvation found in Jesus Christ is a fundamental principle of the Christian faith. Three of the gospel writers report this commission by the Savior. The book of Mark records: *"And he said to them,*

[FINDING THE BALANCE IN WORLD MISSIONS]

'*Go into all the world and proclaim the gospel to the whole creation. Whoever believes and is baptized will be saved, but whoever does not believe will be condemned'*" (Mark 16:15–16). Matthew quotes the Savior's command, "*Go therefore and make disciples of all nations, baptizing them in the name of the Father and of the Son and of the Holy Spirit*" (Matt. 28:19). Luke states, "*Thus it is written, that the Christ should suffer and on the third day rise from the dead, and that repentance and forgiveness of sins should be proclaimed in his name to all nations, beginning from Jerusalem*" (Luke 24:46–47). Applying the Savior's directions in our daily life is a command each of us equally share.

Those in submission to Christ find that Scripture is adamant about our journey being more than going to church, studying the Bible, prayer, short-term mission trips and retreats. We know from Scripture that we are all called to declare Jesus as the hope for the soul and way back to the Father of Creation. The challenge is that some facets of the Church Growth Movement promote the Church as a type of refuge, a social sphere, a place of guidance counseling, a proactive experience among people. All of these are valued qualities but miss what being in Christ is actually about: namely, the death of selfish ambitions and instead living sacrificially for Christ in the spirit of love.

Referencing a few quotes, David Platt in his popular book ***Radical: Taking Back Your Faith from the American Dream***, wrote:

> Have we replaced what is radical about our faith with what is comfortable? Are we settling for Christianity that revolves around catering to ourselves when the central message of Christianity is actually about abandoning ourselves? Radical obedience to Christ is not easy... It's not comfort, not health, not wealth, and not prosperity in this world. Radical obedience to Christ risks losing all these things. But in the end, such risk finds its reward in Christ. And he is more than enough for us.

John Bowen writes in his book *Evangelism for "Normal" People: Good News for Those Looking for a Fresh Approach*:

> For Christians to talk about the gospel is a sign of health; to talk about evangelism is a sign that something is wrong. David Watson says something similar: 'Having to stress the Great Commission, and having to urge people to witness, is not a sign of spiritual life, but a sign of spiritual decadence.'

Charles Finney (1792-1875), a leader in the Second Great Awakening, briefly gives his opinion why Christians are not active in the commission of evangelism:

> It is the great business of every Christian to save souls. People complain that they do not know how to take hold of this matter. Why? The reason is plain enough; they have never studied it. They have never taken the proper pains to qualify themselves for the work. If you do not make it a matter of study, how you may successfully act in building up the kingdom of Christ, you are acting a very wicked and absurd part as a Christian.

It is repeated throughout this book that God has called each Christian to share the gospel in their sphere of influence. This is a mandate that every Christian needs to obey, from the overflow of a new heart. Equally important is the truth that God has called each one of us to participate in cross cultural missions. God has stated and is deeply passionate about seeing His name glorified in every people group on earth.

John Piper states in his 1996 article ***Driving Convictions Behind Foreign Missions***: "When it comes to world missions, there are only three kinds of Christians: <u>zealous goers, zealous senders, and disobedient ones</u>." Some Christians will become zealous goers and long-term cross-cultural missionaries. Those of us who are not zealous goers will instead be zealous senders. The only other option is to be a disobedient Christian, which essentially means that we are not participating in any way in what God is doing around the world to touch the nations.

[FINDING THE BALANCE IN WORLD MISSIONS]

What is a zealous sender? A zealous sender is someone who has come to the realization that they are not called to be a career cross-cultural missionary. However, they have devoted themselves to doing whatever they can to see the great commission fulfilled in other lands. They will intentionally pursue developing relationships and connection with missionaries. They will commit to pray for missionaries and their work. Their sacrificial offerings demonstrate their heart for world evangelization. They will be proactive in participating in local missions, and extend themselves to assist those on the world field so they gain a greater heart for the ministry. A zealous sender is someone who takes personal responsibility and carries a burden for the people groups God has led them to be involved with. A zealous sender says "I'm not called to go at this point in my life, but I'm going to do everything within my power to see the name of Jesus proclaimed among the nations."

Evangelism in essence is not something that we ought to or even need to do. The talk we hear today about reclaiming the Great Commission is based, at least in part, on the assumption that evangelism is a task that we can work ourselves up to, if only we have enough faith or experience. On the contrary, a heart moved to share the gospel is a transformed heart that has encountered the living God.

"It is possible for the most obscure person in a church, with a heart right toward God, to exercise as much power for the evangelization of the world, as it is for those who stand in the most prominent positions." ~ John R. Mott, Chairman of Student Volunteer Movement for foreign missions, 1888.

[13]
A CALL TO REPENTANCE

Jesus was quoted to say in John 17:20, *"I do not ask for these only, but also for those who will believe in me through their word."* We often hear discussions of what is true evangelism. Questions like, "What kind of evangelistic outreach should we have in our day?" The popular notion is that the first obligation of the church is to evangelize the unbelieving. A. W. Tozer, who wrote most eloquently of evangelical concerns as a Christian and as a Missionary Alliance man, the denomination which has more churches in the foreign field than it has in his home country, that the first obligation of the church was not to evangelize but to be spiritually worthy and biblically aligned. He reflected on it well in his book ***Of God and Men***:

> The popular notion that the first obligation of the church is to spread the gospel to the uttermost parts of the earth is false. Her first obligation is to be spiritually worthy to go forth and proclaim it. Our Lord said "Go," but He also said "Wait," and the waiting had to come before the going. Had the disciples gone forth as missionaries before the day of Pentecost, it would have been an overwhelming spiritual disaster, for they could have done no more than make converts after their own likeness, and this would have altered for the worse the whole history of the Western world and had consequences throughout the ages to come. To spread an effete [ineffectual], degenerate brand of Christianity to pagan lands is not to fulfill the commandment of Christ or discharge our obligation to the heathen.

Mr. Tozer went on to say that one of the problems that we have is that the church has become a worldly church as quoted in another book called ***Gems from Tozer: Selections from the Writings of A. W. Tozer***:

In fact it's an accepted part of our way of life. He said our religious mood is social instead of spiritual. We've lost the art of worship. We're not producing saints. Our models are successful businessmen, celebrated athletes, and theological personalities. Our homes have been turned into theatres, our literature is shallow, our hymnody borders on sacrilege, and scarcely anyone appears to care… Increased numbers of demi-Christians is not enough. We need a reformation.

Our Lord's words touch upon this thinking, for He addresses the spread of the testimony of the apostles, and He gives us a very important clue with reference to that which Mr. Tozer is speaking about, how the evangelistic mission is to be carried out in spirit and in truth.

Jesus also spoke of the corrupted hearts found in leaders then and now, saying *"Woe to you… hypocrites! For you travel across sea and land to make a single convert, and when he becomes a convert, you make him twice as much a child of hell as yourselves"* (Matt. 23:15). To be a child of hell was a Hebrew phrase, signifying to be deserving of hell, to be horribly wicked.

The Jewish sect called the Pharisees sought converts to either grow their followers' numbers or to obtain money by extorting donations under various pretenses. They were very busy turning souls to become dedicated to their persuasion as a person might lure souls to a preferred church or organization for vanities sake. They were not motivated for the glory of God and the good of souls, but that they might have the credit and advantage of making converts for their cause. Their temporal gain was their fruit of godliness, by use of a thousand devices they use religion to pave the way for their worldly interests. They were very strict and precise in smaller matters of the law, but careless and loose in important matters. While they would seem to be godly, they were neither contrite nor righteous.

When they had accomplished their own purpose, they took no care to instruct the converts or to guide them. The

[A Call to Repentance]

righteousness of the scribes and Pharisees was like new clothes to dress a cadaver, only for show without life. It is the just nature of God to give those corrupt up to their hearts' lusts, who obstinately persist in gratifying them. Christ gives men over to their true characters. Such is the misconduct sometimes found on the mission field today, specifically in poor countries, where desperate needs inspire desperate measures.

Every highly attuned mission's organization must constantly filter out self-proclaimed native pastors who are opportunists, using the Christian message for personal gain. Paul warned Timothy of this in 1 Timothy 6:5: *"constant friction among people who are depraved in mind and deprived of the truth, imagining that godliness is a means of gain."* From an unregenerate position, some men use the gospel to solicit money for personal purposes.

In 2011, The Telegraph in the UK reported an Indian missionary named Dr. P.P. Job, who falsely portrayed young Buddhist girls from Nepal as orphans of murdered Christians in a global fund-raising operation involving British and American churches. The charity claimed they had been either abandoned by their parents who did not want the financial burden of raising girls, or orphaned after their allegedly Christian parents were murdered by Nepal's Maoist insurgents. Many of the donors were in the United States, Holland and Britain, where Dr. Job's sister organization raised around $30,000 USD for the Michael Job Centre between 2007 and 2010. Thanks to an anti-trafficking charity run by an unnamed retired British Army officer, who assisted Indian officials in a raid on the Coimbatore center, where 23 children were rescued.

Another disturbing and bizarre account was that of Paul Henry Dean, an Australian businessman who suddenly left family, friends and middle class comforts for a new life among lepers, orphans and the desperately poor of India. Dean donned an array of names and identities while he operated as a charity worker, masqueraded as a holy man and a healer, and allegedly abused dozens of boys and young men in his wanderings over 30 years. He travelled the countryside pretending to be a Catholic brother and a priest, operating with impunity, and descending upon charities that worked with orphans. Dean has been a living plague of iniquity, changing countries, moving from state to state, from one charity to another.

From the arena of native missions, there have been many self-appointed pastors who have learned effective techniques and continue to hone them with skill, using social sites on the Internet to lure the empathetic and trusting. They may grow followers to impress donors, with the intent to extort donations for their own needs, while scantily providing for those depicted in photos as the needy. These opportunists often share emotionally manipulating photos to appeal to the beguiled, empathetic Christians who cannot differentiate a deceiver from a genuine servant of God. These men and women may plant a few village churches and stage outreaches, but their overarching motive will be to satisfy their personal finances and their family's needs.

There are also examples where 10 to 20 family members will buy a banner and write "Christ Church of a [insert a City]" and proceed to email and post photos on US and European websites, searching for support money to finance their fictitious or actual church plant. Depending on with whom they are communicating; Catholic, Charismatic, Protestant, even cults and false teachers, these self-appointed pastors will adjust their theology or belief in order to encourage and maximize their financial support. Some of these indigenous church fronts who claim to manage orphanages don't actually have any resident orphans, but rather dirty up local village children with family nearby, to pose for petitioning photos.

On the donor's end, many Christians in prosperous nations have rarely learned to give sacrificially, but consider their

[A Call to Repentance]

own welfare first, giving meagerly out of their abundance. Prosperity should lead to generosity, for the Scripture says that God makes people wealthy so that they can be generous—that is one of the purposes of the wealth (2 Cor. 9:11). But ironically, the Scripture also says that wealth often has an adverse effect on the wealthy, making them less generous rather than more. Thus, although wealthy people should be rich toward God, they are often rich toward themselves instead, where many will not enter the Kingdom of God (Luke 18:18-25, 16:19-31). But this result is not unavoidable. When wealthy people are radically changed by the gospel, they become generous in the way God intends. In other words, prosperity can lead to generosity, when God's grace is present.

To the sin of mission organizations, there are those who desire to control nationals by the purse-strings and falsely use the term "accountability" to dictate specific local strategies and specific local priorities, rather than merely insuring the general trustworthy use of funds. Additionally, some supporting churches will see nothing wrong with preaching against hirelings in one breath and then demanding obedience from indigenous evangelists in very specific local decision-making processes, something better left to the people knowing the cultural milieu of ministry on-site.

What's to be done about all this error and deception among God's children? Proclaim the urgency for repentance among all those in Christ. Submit to fasting with prayer, motivated by an earnest seeking to return to the course—all of us. Ask the Lord for wisdom, to discern deceptive motives. We all can stray; anyone can deceive and be deceived. Today is a new day, an opportunity to change direction. Without exclusivity, every transformed Christian is charged by the Great Commission to either go, work or support: *"Therefore go and make disciples of all nations, baptizing them in the name of the Father and of the Son and of the Holy Spirit, and teaching them to obey everything I have commanded you"*

(Matt. 28:18-20). Also, in Acts 1:8, Luke echoes the Lord's words to Theophilus, saying *"you will be my witnesses in Jerusalem and in all Judea and Samaria, and to the end of the earth."*

Yes, we all need to humbly repent from deceptive motivations or unwise choices, submitting our lives daily to the Lord. The best of intentions can be deceptively corrupt, whereas *"The heart is deceitful above all things and beyond cure. Who can understand it?"* (Jeremiah 17:9). Our susceptibility to being inwardly deceived is a sobering fact, whereas the path is wide that is lined with deception and strayed souls, but walking in the way of God's counsel is narrow and entering the gate is difficult (Matt. 7:13-14).

As we have already discussed in this book, humanism strives to provide social relief as an end solution for all of humanity's suffering. What is different from the motivation of a genuinely transformed Christian is the urgent need to share the hope found in Christ Jesus – that none shall pass into eternity, to enter into the peace of God, unless they have accepted Jesus.

[14]
THE SCRIPTURES AND EVANGELISM

A discussion regarding Evangelism would not be complete without referencing the unequivocal authority and direction behind it. The Bible provides the clear principles of evangelism, as both the message and the method are found in Scripture. Bible principles are applicable to every age in every culture, and should direct the method of evangelism. It is the record of God's revelation of Himself to His people, which presents the goals of evangelism and is the dynamic for it. Without dispute, authentic evangelism must be based upon the Word of God.

Today as never before, Christians are being crossed-examine and scrutinized as to give reasons for the hope that is within them. Often in the evangelistic context seekers raise questions about the validity of the gospel message. Removing intellectual objections will not make anyone become a Christian; a change of heart inspired by the Spirit is necessary. While intellectual reasoning by Scripture alone is not sufficient to bring another to Christ, it does not follow that it is unnecessary. The place and purpose of apologetics in the sharing of our faith with others is essential.

The word "apologetics" never appears in the Bible, but there is a verse which contains its meaning: *"But in your hearts revere Christ as Lord. Always be prepared to give an answer to everyone who asks you to give the reason for the hope that you have. But do this with gentleness and respect..."* (1 Peter 3:15). The Greek word *apologia* means "answer," or "reasonable defense." It does not mean to apologize, nor does it mean only engage in intellectual dialogue. It means to provide reasonable answers to honest questions and to do it with humility, respect, and reverence. The verse thus suggests that the manner in which one applies apologetics is as important as the words expressed. Peter tells us in this passage that Christians are to be ready always with answers for those who inquire of us concerning our faith.

The very reason why Christians are put in the position of giving a reasoned account of the hope that is found in them is that not all men have faith. Because there is a world to be evangelized, there is the need for the believer to defend their faith: Evangelism by its very nature brings one into apologetics. Because of this, we can reason that apologetics is not a mere matter of "intellectual jousting"; it is a serious matter of eternal life and death.

Those who follow the intellectual principle of neutrality and the epistemological method of unbelieving scholarship do not follow nor conform to the sovereign Lordship of God. As a result, their reasoning is made vain (Rom. 1:21). In Ephesians 4, Paul prohibits the Christian from following this vain mindset. Paul goes on to teach that the believer's thinking is in reverse contrast to the ignorant and darkened thinking of the Gentiles. *"But you did not learn Christ after this manner!"* (Eph. 4:20). Unlike the Gentiles (unregenerate) who are alienated from the life of God, the Christian has put away the old nature and has been *"...renewed in the spirit of your minds"* (Eph. 4:23). The Christian is inwardly different from the world; he or she does not follow the neutral methods of unbelief, but by God's grace we have a new commitment and a way of thinking.

Christianity expresses itself properly with intelligence, not ignorance. If a Reformation is to accompany the revival for which many of us pray, it must be something of the mind as well as the heart. We are to love God with the mind as well as the heart and the soul. It was Jesus who said, *"Come and see."* He invites our scrutiny and investigation both before and after conversion. Matt. 13:23 reads, *"But he who received the seed on the good ground is he who hears the* *word and <u>understands</u> it, who indeed bears fruit.*" They all heard it, but only the "good soil" <u>comprehended</u> it.

In Acts 8:30, Luke wrote, "*When the Spirit prompted Philip to join himself to the chariot of the Ethiopian eunuch (who was reading Isaiah 53), he asked, 'Do you <u>understand</u> what you are reading?' The eunuch replied, 'How can I except some man should guide me?'*" Again in Acts 18:4 we read that Paul at Corinth was "*<u>reasoning</u> in the synagogue every Sabbath and trying to <u>persuade</u> the Jews and Greeks.*" While there are other verses, we will look at 2 Cor. 5:11, which reads, "*We <u>persuade</u> men,*" states Paul. Vine's Expository Dictionary describes this Greek word like this: "to apply persuasion, to prevail upon or win over, bringing about a change of mind by the influence of reason or moral considerations."

All of these words—persuasion, dialogue, discourse, dispute, argue, present evidence, reason with—are vehicles of communication and are at the heart of Paul's classical evangelistic model. Can there be saving faith without understanding? Can there be understanding without reasoning? The Scripture would seem to stress that these are all important components. Paul urges believers in 2 Tim. 2:15 to study to show ourselves approved unto God, workmen that need not to be ashamed. Sharing the gospel involves communication from a full and proper understanding of Scripture. People must be focused upon and then understand the gospel to respond to it. It is our responsibility as Christians to make it as clear as possible for all who will listen. "*Knowing, therefore, the terror of the Lord, we persuade men*" (2 Cor. 5:11).

Native missionary Dr. Rochunga Pudaite is the founder of "Bibles for the World." His tribe, called the Hmar is located in northeast India, came to know the gospel through the influence of Watkin Roberts, a missionary from Wales. As a result of the missionary's sacrificial work, Rochunga Pudaite's father proceeded to memorize the entire Gospel of John. It was the only part of the Bible he had access to. He memorized it because he was afraid he would forget it. To retain it, he would recite it over and over again. In fact, everywhere he went he would quote from the Book of John. It was through his sharing of the Gospel of John that the Holy Spirit reached that tribe of approximately 100,000 Indians. Rochunga Pudaite's father became known as the "Walking Gospel of John" whose life and message had a profound impact on the Hmar people. Him knowing the Scripture, even if only a segment, was sufficient for yielding mighty works for the glory of God.

Isaiah 55:11 most eloquently states, *"so shall my word be that goes out from my mouth; it shall not return to me empty, but it shall accomplish that which I purpose, and shall succeed in the thing for which I sent it."* God's word is unique. It was by His uttered word that God created: *"God said, 'Let there be light'; and there was light"* (Genesis 1:3). *"By faith we understand that the worlds were prepared by the Word of God"* (Hebrews 11:3). Again we are encouraged in Deut. 32:2: *"May my teaching drop as the rain, my speech distill as the dew, like gentle rain upon the tender grass, and like showers upon the herb."* The Scripture as a whole emanates the very essence of God's person as light and life-giving substance for the soul.

Jesus used the Scriptures in conversation with individuals as well as in His teaching. In the synagogue in Nazareth, Jesus was found reading the Tanakh (Masoretic Text or Hebrew Scriptures). After reading Isaiah 61:1-2, he began to explain to his hearers how the Scriptures were being fulfilled (Luke 4:16-21). Jesus' basic approach to preaching and teaching was an explanation of the Scriptures. After the resurrection, Jesus walked with two of His disciples to Emmaus, *"And beginning at Moses and all the prophets, he expounded unto them in all the Scriptures the things concerning himself"* (Luke 24:27). He used illustrations,

[THE SCRIPTURES IN EVANGELISM]

parables, object lessons, current events, and questions, all to help the hearer understand the Word of God.

The substance of Scripture bases some of its main arguments on the evidence provided by the material world. Reading 2 Peter 1:16-21. It starts out, *"For we did not follow cleverly devised myths when we made known to you the power and coming of our Lord Jesus Christ, but we were eyewitnesses of his majesty."* The writer here points out that the person and work of Christ is not based on the beliefs of what people construed. The gospel revealing the person and office of Jesus is largely based on what happened in the physical world, as seen by witnesses. What historically took place actually happened, and no personal beliefs one way or the other could alter the facts. And these facts, which speak for themselves, says Peter in verses 20 and 21, verify the testimony of Scripture.

We can surmise that Scripture sets a witnessing example for us that not only allows us to use evidence from the material world, but shows us by example, when it is our responsibility to do so. While the truths of Christianity will exist eternally beyond the scope of creation, our faith is not so utterly ostentatious that it is reduced to an opinion that has little impact on our world.

Evangelism through teaching has not changed over the centuries, although people do go to great lengths to modify it. The teacher who would properly evangelize his listener must explain the revelation of Scripture clearly concerning the redemptive work of Christ. The Holy Spirit provides the spiritual understanding, but He does it through the oracles of inspired Scripture. Successful evangelism through the good news occurs when the Spirit of God empowers the Word of Truth through the evangelist to reach the heart of the unconverted soul. The truths found in the Bible are exacting words shared by the evangelist to bring hope and conviction to the unconverted, just as medicine may be the means used by a doctor to restore health to the sick.

Conviction of sin comes through the Scriptures and it is the first work of the Spirit upon a soul: *"For the word of God is living and active, sharper than any two-edged sword, piercing to the division of soul and of spirit, of joints and of marrow, and discerning the thoughts and intentions of the heart"* (Heb. 4:12). The revealed truth found in Scripture lays bare the sin that is hidden in the mind and hearts of humanity. The Word of God convicts by illuminating the mind concerning known and hidden sin and shows an individual his or her reprobate condition. However, most unbelievers have hearts hardened by the deceitfulness of sin: *"Is not my word like fire, declares the LORD, and like a hammer that breaks the rock in pieces?"* (Jeremiah 23:29). God's Word brings conviction even to the hardest heart and causes the person to comprehend how he falls short of God's divine attribute of holiness.

J. I. Packer in his book ***Evangelism and the Sovereignty of God*** states that "To be convicted of sin means [...] to realize that one had offended God and flouted his authority, and defied him and gone against him." Because of rebellion, men and women stand condemned under God's holy precepts. Conviction is evidenced when the concerned person becomes aware of his or her wrong relationship with God, and sees the need to enter into a regenerated relationship with Him. Packer further states that "Conviction of sin always includes an understanding of sins: a sense of guilt for particular wrongs done in the sight of God." We see ourselves as apart from God and recognizing the result of specific sinful actions, are moved to anguish and sorrow. "Conviction always includes conviction of sinfulness: a sense of one's complete corruption and perversity in God's sight."

No pastor, teacher or evangelist can by force or logical manipulation, bring conviction by the utterance of Scripture alone. There is a need for a supernaturally transformed heart because of the utter corruption of the sinner in God's sight. This transformation is wrought not only by the discourse of

[THE SCRIPTURES IN EVANGELISM]

Scripture alone, but in combination and empowerment of the Spirit moving upon the soul to deposit the seed of life. Paul stated it well in his letter to the Corinthians, *"I planted [the seed], Apollos watered, but God gave the growth. So neither he who plants nor he who waters is anything, but only God who gives the growth"* (1 Cor. 3:6-7).

The Scripture is said to convert a soul: *"The law of the Lord is perfect, reviving the soul; the testimony of the Lord is sure, making wise the simple"* (Psalms 19:7). This conversion results in a changed heart within the penitent. The source of this changed life is again realized through the life-giving revelations found in the Scriptures. The converted person turns around in his or her path of life through repentance and starts walking in God's direction. The soul-winner engaged in evangelism should make certain that the truths of Scripture are understood and communicated clearly. It is not illustration, rational process, nor forceful logic that wins souls. Strategy, intellectual manipulation and salesmanship are not the tools of God. Only by the Word of God through the Holy Spirit can God move in conviction and thus conversion.

God also uses the Scripture to breathe hope and inspire rebirth for the soul. When a person is born the first time, he or she is given earthly life. Jesus said to Nicodemus, *"Do not marvel that I said to you, 'You must be born again'"* (John 3:7). When a person is born the second time, he or she is given eternal life. God uses the Scripture as an instrument through which to give eternal life to seeking souls. Peter recognized the Bible as the living declaration of eternal life: *"you have been born again, not of perishable seed but of imperishable, through the living and abiding word of God"* (1 Peter 1:23). Therefore, it is through the conveyance of Scripture that the Holy Spirit can move a sinner to receive eternal life.

"Jesus is God" is a powerful truth relevant to effective evangelism: *"In the beginning was the Word, and the Word was with God, and the Word was God"* (John 1:1). When He was upon the earth, He spoke many things. Jesus indicated His words were instruments through which the Holy Spirit could give life: *"It is the Spirit who gives life; the flesh is no help at all. The words that I have spoken to you are spirit and life"* (John 6:63). The truth found in the Bible gives life, when it was spoken by Jesus upon the earth and later written to create the words of Scripture.

The truth found in Scripture brings cleansing. *"Already you are clean because of the word that I have spoken to you"* (John 15:3). The Lord here expressly states that cleansing from sin comes through the holy Word. Jesus speaks of *"abiding in me"* (KJV vs. 4) as the appropriation of cleansing. People are not forgiven just because they hear the Word of God but there must be an ongoing appropriation of it. In other words, the hearer must daily apply what he or she learns as life-giving truth or the understanding will become unprofitable (James 1:24). The teacher-evangelist, therefore, must communicate clearly the precepts of God's eternal counsel in order that the teaching can be understood and applied.

The Scriptures deliver the seeds of faith unto salvation: *"So faith comes from hearing, and hearing through the word of Christ"* (Romans 10:17). The Bible is a sure foundation upon which one may root his or her faith. Apart from the solid truths found in Scripture, there can be no ground or framework for faith. However, one cannot make the Scripture the foundation of one's faith unless he or she hears and comprehends the meaning of the Scripture. The message must be received and genuinely believed in order for it to be operative in the life of an individual. The stability of any convert's faith comes from the whole revelation, based upon the written Word of Truth.

Sanctification means "to set apart to God," "to make holy." The Word of God is the means through which the convert may be sanctified. Our Lord in His high priestly prayer

[THE SCRIPTURES IN EVANGELISM]

asked, *"Sanctify them in the truth; your word is truth"* (John 17:17). Christ also gave Himself for the Church, *"that he might sanctify her, having cleansed her by the washing of water with the word"* (Ephesians 5:26). Therefore along with cleansing His Church from the guilt and power of sin through regeneration or the washing of water, the Scripture is also an instrument through which the believer is cleansed from inherited sin or made holy.

What is the gospel? In 1 Cor. 15:1-8 the apostle Paul summarizes the most basic ingredients of the gospel message, namely, the death, burial, resurrection, and appearances of the resurrected Christ. These verses, which were an early Christian confession, provide for us the heart of the gospel and show us that each listed attribute is an integral part of the gospel. Note that Paul described these as *"of first importance"*—a phrase that stresses priority, not time. The stress is on the centrality of these truths to the gospel message. The complete gospel is indeed a powerful message of salvation to sinners. The gospel of God is His revelation of redemption. If you know that the Word of God will accomplish what God wants it to and if you know that the gospel has power to save, then it should give you boldness to know that in witnessing you are using two very powerful tools: God's Word and God's gospel.

John 12:32 quotes Jesus, saying *"And I, if I be lifted up from the earth, will draw all men to myself."* Here Jesus speaks specifically about His crucifixion. It is He who draws to Himself all who are to be saved. When we present the gospel (1 Cor. 15:1-4), the sacrificial death and resurrection of Jesus for sins, Jesus draws the sinner to Himself. The Holy Spirit does the work; we are only conveyors of the message. We deliver the good news. *"How shall they believe in Him who they have not heard?"* (Romans 10:14).

The evangelist (including every Christian) must learn the Scripture accurately and thoroughly. They must also have experienced its power in their own life, and must be convinced: *"For I am not ashamed of the gospel, for it is the power of God for salvation to everyone who believes, to the Jew first and also to the Greek"* (Romans 1:16). The evangelist also must accept it as infallible and authoritative in Spirit and truth: *"All Scripture is breathed out by God and profitable for teaching, for reproof, for correction, and for training in righteousness"* (2 Timothy 3:16). The teacher didactically delivers God's Word and through it the Holy Spirit speaks to the seeking soul and enlightens their hearts. There is no other book ordained by God upon which the teacher can rely to change the lives of others. The revelation from Scripture is relevant to the needs and situations of each person today.

"The concern for world evangelization is not something tacked on to a man's personal Christianity, which he may take or leave as he chooses. It is rooted in the character of the God who has come to us in Christ Jesus. Thus, it can never be the province of a few enthusiasts, a sideline or a specialty of those who happen to have a bent that way. It is the distinctive mark of being a Christian." ~ James S. Stewart, Former Moderator of the General Assembly of the Church of Scotland (1963-64).

[15]
THE HOLY SPIRIT IN EVANGELISM

We have already determined in previous chapters that the unsaved person is unable to discern the meaning of the gospel by intellectual reasoning. The Scriptures teach that Satan has blinded the unsaved person, rendering him or her incapable of perceiving the good news: *"And even if our gospel is veiled, it is veiled to those who are perishing. In their case the god of this world has blinded the minds of the unbelievers, to keep them from seeing the light of the gospel of the glory of Christ, who is the image of God"* (2 Cor. 4:3-4). Because of this, unsaved people do not realize their lost condition. Even when they are warned of the judgment of God to come, they have little concern due to no ability to comprehend. An indifferent and neglectful attitude toward eternity is common among sin-hardened hearts.

The teaching that is effective for evangelism must have a dynamic far greater than the communication of biblical facts and practical illustrations. The mechanics of teaching can be little more than the impersonal details to be followed in the classroom. The dynamic for effective biblical teaching is the Holy Spirit who empowers the Word and the work. Apart from His ministry, the evangelist's best intentions, motives, and methods will fall woefully short of what God intended. When teaching under the influence of the Holy Spirit, the teacher will realize results that transform lives for Christ, for He is the empowering agent of evangelism.

Dr. Johannes Blauw of the Netherlands Missionary Council, reports in the 1962 release of **Missionary Nature of the Church** about dependence on the Holy Spirit as the guide in evangelism. He writes:

Let us not forget that the great prime mover of the preaching of the gospel does not come from outside (the "need of the world") and not from within either (the "religious impulse") but from above, as a divine coercion *"woe is unto me, if I preach not the gospel!"* (1 Cor. 9:16), as a matter of life and death, not for the world, but for the Church itself *"And this I do for the gospel's sake, that I might be partaker thereof with you"* (1 Cor. 9: 23). This enduring presence of Christ in and through the Holy Spirit is to enable the disciples now in their turn to carry out the commission to preach the gospel to all nations. Emphasis is rightly laid by all sorts of publications on the fact that Christ Himself does His work of proclamation of the gospel through the Holy Spirit. He charges them to mission, certainly, but He does not delegate it to them. It is solely by the authority of the Holy Spirit that the disciples will be in a position to be witnesses of Christ to the uttermost parts of the earth, Acts 1: 6-8 (cf. Luke 24: 47 and John 20: 21).

Before a person can be converted, the gospel must be understood by the heart. The Holy Spirit's office in part is to convict the world of sin, *"And when he comes, he will convict the world concerning sin and righteousness and judgment"* (John 16:8). Conviction is more than sorrow for sins, although that may follow. Conviction awakens the mind concerning the truth, namely our position before God. The Holy Spirit causes the sinner to see that they are guilty before God, having broken His laws, unable to function in the correct spirit of love. Our eyes are opened to how grievously frail our condition is, that we cannot in ourselves measure up to His perfect standard. We read, *"...for all have sinned and fall short of the glory of God"* (Rom. 3:23). Conviction causes the sinner to realize he has not believed in Christ, *"concerning sin, because they do not believe in me"* (John 16:9).

From Oswald Chambers compilation of lectures forming **My Utmost For His Highest** we read:

> Conviction of sin is one of the rarest things that ever strikes a man. It is the threshold of an understanding of God. Jesus

[THE HOLY SPIRIT IN EVANGELISM]

Christ said that when the Holy Spirit came He would convict of sin, and when the Holy Spirit rouses the conscience and brings him into the presence of God, it is not his relationship with men that bothers him, but his relationship with God.

The unsaved person will remain in a lost, sinful condition if he or she rejects the Son of God: *"Whoever believes in him is not condemned, but whoever does not believe is condemned already, because he has not believed in the name of the only Son of God"* (John 3:18). All people are sinners, but Christ died for all people. The main issue facing the sinner is what to do with Jesus? When the Holy Spirit convicts of unrighteousness, *"And when he comes, he will convict the world concerning sin and righteousness and judgment"* (John 16:8), he will cause people to see Jesus Christ as the only righteous one (John 16:10). Only the work of the Holy Spirit can cause the unconverted to understand that the righteous Christ died for the unrighteous person.

A person unaided by spiritual enlightenment cannot understand his or her condition before God, because he or she does not comprehend spiritual truth: *"The natural person does not accept the things of the Spirit of God, for they are folly to him, and he is not able to understand them because they are spiritually discerned"* (1 Cor. 2:14). Additionally, the Holy Spirit convicts of judgment (John 16:8). This passage refers to God's judgment on sin at the death of Christ (John 12:31-32; 2 Cor. 5:21). When the Holy Spirit convicts concerning judgment, the sinner understands that Christ's death was a judgment upon the sinner's sin.

Regeneration is the work of the Holy Spirit whereby life is imparted in response to faith. The Scriptures point out that humanity is spiritually dead and separated from God by sin: *"even when we were dead in our trespasses, made us alive together with Christ—by grace you have been saved"* (Ephesians 2:5). By the miracle of regeneration, the soul is given eternal life. Our Lord describes this granting of eternal life as being "born again" (John 3:3). The Holy Spirit is the one who gives life to the soul when a person believes and places his or her faith in Jesus Christ.

Good intentions cannot make a person desire to consider, much less seek, regeneration. The Holy Spirit must work in the heart as the gospel is heard and believed. As the new birth takes place, eternal life is imparted. *"Whoever believes in the Son has eternal life; whoever does not obey the Son shall not see life, but the wrath of God remains on him"* (John 3:36); *"he saved us, not because of works done by us in righteousness, but according to his own mercy, by the washing of regeneration and renewal of the Holy Spirit"* (Titus 3:5).

Dwight L. Moody, in his book **Secret Power**, wrote, "I believe that many a man is praying for God to fill him when he is full already with something else. Before we pray that God would fill us, we ought to pray Him to empty us." Since the beginning of the Church age, the Church has always had to rely on God's Spirit to provide an empowered witness. Our efforts at evangelism are often, at best, an exercise in recruitment. When energized by the Holy Spirit, however, evangelism becomes sharing the good news in an inhumanely powerful and comprehensible way as the Holy Spirit opens peoples' hearts.

The promise of Scripture is clear: when a soul comes to the saving knowledge of Jesus Christ, the Holy Spirit comes to dwell within that person (Eph. 1:13-14). As a result, they receive "power" from God's Holy Spirit, to complete the task given them to accomplish (1 Cor. 12:7). Along with the power, the Spirit gives "gift(s)" for the believer to complete the task. The purpose of the gift(s) is not for us to merely have a supernatural ability, but for us to use this new ability to accomplish the work assigned for us. The gifts given by the Holy Spirit and His abiding presence are intended to accomplish the work of the Spirit, equipping the believer.

Consider carefully the very last words which our Lord spoke as He met with His disciples on the Mount of Olives only moments before He ascended into heaven. Jesus had commissioned His disciples to go into all the world and preach the gospel and to make disciples of all nations (Matt. 28:19). But He had told them not to leave Jerusalem until they were filled with the power of the Holy Spirit (Acts 1:4). *"You will receive power,"* He said, *"when the Holy Spirit has come upon you, and you will be my witnesses in Jerusalem and in all Judea and Samaria, and to the end of the earth"* (Acts 1:8).

By these words, Jesus was suggesting, "Though you have been with Me these three plus years, it is not enough that you have heard Me teach the profound truths, and have seen Me heal the sick and raise the dead. You need to be empowered with the Holy Spirit in order to be effective and fruitful as My witnesses throughout the world." Indeed, the Christian life is a great adventure if we submit to God's ways. It is a life of purpose and power. Christ has given us a profound promise, *"Truly, truly, I say to you, whoever believes in me will also do the works that I do; and greater works than these will he do, because I am going to the Father. Whatever you ask in my name, this I will do, that the Father may be glorified in the Son. If you ask me anything in my name, I will do it"* (John 14:12-13).

In Matt. 4:19, Jesus said to his followers, *"Follow me, and I will make you fishers of men."* First century Christians, controlled and empowered by the Holy Spirit and filled with His love, turned the known world upside down. As the disciples were filled with the Holy Spirit, they received a divine, supernatural power that changed them from fearful men to radiant witnesses for Christ. However today, multitudes of Christians do not know who the Holy Spirit is by biblical definition. Or, if they do, they do not know how to appropriate His power. Consequently, they go through life without ever experiencing the abundant and fruitful life which Christ promised to all who trust Him.

With a discerning heart, we are reminded of the great contrast between the post-modern Church today and the Church in the first century. In his 1947 introduction to the book *Letters to the Young Churches*, J.B. Phillips writes:

> The great difference between present-day Christianity and that of which we read in these letters, the New Testament epistles, is that to us, it is primarily a performance; to them it was a real experience. We are apt to reduce the Christian religion to a code or, at best, a rule of heart and life. To these men it is quite plainly the invasion of their lives by a new quality of life together. They do not hesitate to describe this as Christ living in them.

Eph. 5:18 teaches us to *"be filled with the Spirit."* To live a Spirit-filled life means to yield ourselves to the control of the Holy Spirit. The way to do that is to *"let the word of Christ richly dwell within you"* (Col. 3:16). Being filled with the Spirit and letting the Word dwell in you are synonymous because they produce the same results: a song in your heart, a thankful attitude, and loving relationships in all environments (Eph. 5:19--6:9; Col. 3:16--4:1). God can do great things through you.

Eph. 3:20 says He *"...is able to do far more abundantly beyond all that we ask or think, according to the power that works within us."* The power is in you by promise; it simply needs to be released. This happens when we yield every aspect of our life to the Spirit's dominion. In Galatians 5:16-18 we are given the command to obey the Spirit, not the flesh. *"But I say, walk by the Spirit, and do not gratify the desires of the flesh. For the desires of the flesh are against the Spirit, and the desires of the Spirit are against the flesh; for these are opposed to each other, to prevent you from doing what you would."*

However, submission and empowerment alone is not all, but intrinsically, we must have Godly compassion for lost people which is an essential component to evangelism. The Holy Spirit must fill believers with His compassion. The old-time Pentecostals spoke of having a burden for the lost. Weeping and crying at the altar because of lost people should be something we experience, not something we read about in Church history books. The passion of the Spirit can empower us with the compassion of Jesus to reach the lost. We must specifically petition the Lord to change our hearts, to help us genuinely love others. Depending on our journey in life, this may be a difficult transition to allow.

One of the great preachers in U.S. history is Dwight L. Moody. He pastored in Chicago, leaving a Bible College as a monument that bears his name and values. Mr. Moody was a successful minister, but by his own admission, he lacked power in his ministry. One day two women came up to him after a service. They said, "We have been praying for you."

"Why don't you pray for the people?" he asked.

"Because you need the power of the Spirit," they said.

"I need the power! Why?" said Mr. Moody

Moody writes, "I thought I had power. I had the largest congregation in Chicago, and there were many conversions." He also said that in a sense, he was satisfied with where he was at. But these two praying women changed his course. They told him that they were praying for an anointing by the Holy Spirit. Mr. Moody could not get this off his mind and he wrote, "There came a great hunger in my soul. I did not know what it was and I began to cry out to God as never before. I felt I did not want to live if I could not have this power for service."

Rev. Moody withdrew for a time, praying, and sought fervently to be filled by God's power. He writes the following: "Well, one day, in the city of New York -- oh, what a day! -- I cannot describe it, I seldom refer to it; it is almost too sacred an experience to name. Paul had an experience of which he never spoke for fourteen years. I can only say that God revealed Himself to me, and I had such an experience of His love that I had to ask Him to stay His hand. I went to preaching again. The sermons were not different; I did not present any new truths, and yet hundreds were converted. I would not now be placed back where I was before that blessed experience if you should give me all the world."

When the Word of God is faithfully shared in truth, the Holy Spirit uses the Word and applies God's message to the need and situation of the listener. The Holy Spirit impresses upon the person that there is no other source of salvation except through the blood of Jesus Christ. As the Word is faithfully taught in the Spirit, the spiritual eyes of the unsaved are unveiled by means of God's life changing truths. Converts are enlightened through the working of the Holy Spirit, regarding their sin, Christ's righteousness, and the judgment of sin. *"For everyone who does wicked things hates the light and does not come to the light, lest his works should be exposed"* (John 3:20).

The Holy Spirit is the agent, carrying out salvation in every heart. Halford Edward Luccock, American Methodist minister and professor of Homiletics at Yale's Divinity School in the early 1900's correctly observed, "The Holy Spirit is the present tense of God." God is presently working in the hearts and lives of every individual being called through the person of the Holy Spirit. The actual transformation of any listener will come as God's Spirit moves in their hearts.

[16]
PRAYER ESSENTIAL FOR EVANGELISM

Prayer is absolutely essential to the spiritual life and in evangelism. Prayer is the cry of the soul to God. It is opening one's heart to God as one opens his heart to a friend, involving intimacy, trust and understanding. The Christian who is the mightiest in their closets with God are the mightiest in their outreach with souls.

Every great awakening in the history of the Church from the time of the Apostles until present time has been the result of fervent prayer. There have been great awakenings without much preaching, and there have been great awakenings with absolutely no organization, but there has never been a true awakening without intentional prayer. Without periodic, extraordinary visitations of God, the church inevitably degenerates.

"The Great Awakening" in the 18th century, in which Jonathan Edwards was one of the accepted central figures, began with his famous "Call to Prayer." The work of David Brainerd among the North American Indians, one of the greatest works in all history, had its origin in the days and nights that Brainerd spent before God in prayer for an endowment of power from on high for his work among the natives. In 1830 there was a revival in Rochester, New York, in which Charles G. Finney was the outstanding human agent. This revival spread throughout that region of the state and 100,000 persons were reported as having connected themselves with the churches as the result of this work. The great Welsh revival in 1904 and 1905 was unquestionably the outcome of prayer as was the Chile revival in 1909.

The Church has long been engaged in the work of evangelism, with all it demands and sacrifices. However, it has not always combined the work of evangelism with the devotion of earnest prayer. This oversight may account for much of the failure of many well-meaning evangelistic efforts. Attempts to be fruitful in evangelism or any other function in the Church with minimal prayer will yield limited fruit. Without prayer, God's people often lack the transformed hearts filled with compassion and the conviction, both essential to be effective. If God is not earnestly sought to touch the heart of the unbeliever as He promises to do in response to our prayers, we will turn to human resources and human understanding. Soul winning requires the supernatural power of God to release those who are in Satan's grip (Matt. 17:21) and to open the eyes of those blinded to the light of the gospel (2 Cor. 4:4).

Edward McKendree Bounds writes in his book ***Power Through Prayer***:

> It is necessary to iterate and reiterate that prayer, as a mere habit, as a performance gone through by routine or in a professional way, is a dead and rotten thing. Such praying has no connection with the praying for which we plead. We are stressing true praying, which engages and sets on fire every high element of the preacher's being -- prayer which is born of vital oneness with Christ and the fullness of the Holy Ghost, which springs from the deep, overflowing fountains of tender compassion, deathless solicitude for man's eternal good; a consuming zeal for the glory of God; a thorough conviction of the preacher's difficult and delicate work and of the imperative need of God's mightiest help. Praying grounded on these solemn and profound convictions is the only true praying. Preaching backed by such praying is the only preaching which sows the seeds of eternal life in human hearts and builds men up for heaven.

Prayer is pivotal and essential, whereas nothing of spiritual depth can develop within us or though us without prayer. The evangelist is commissioned by God to daily fervent prayer as well as to declare the good news with all boldness. The evangelist may speak with the eloquence of humanity

[Prayer Essential for Evangelism]

and with the voice of angels, but unless he or she prays for daily transformation and empowerment which draws sinning souls heavenward, the preaching will be *"as sounding brass or a tinkling cymbal"* (1 Cor. 13:1). God calls His people to prayer with a passion combined with an abiding intimacy in Christ, which springs from an overflowing heart of compassion and a consuming zeal for the love and the glory of God. Such does not come by mere self-will or intentional striving, but by surrender of heart and soul to the vine of Christ, seeking daily a new transformation from the purification work of the Master.

"Your kingdom come, your will be done, on earth as it is in heaven" (Matt. 6:10). These words from the prayer Jesus taught his disciples express God's plan and purpose in this world. They bring together in the simplest and most powerful way prayer in evangelism. The compelling vision of the Kingdom of God draws us into a deeper commitment to Jesus as Lord of our lives. It calls us to truly repent, turn from our own agenda and fully embrace His call of unreserved devotion and submission. We are challenged to open our hearts to the renewing and empowering of his Holy Spirit, to be transformed into His likeness and to go into the world and make disciples.

God has something very great to accomplish through His church, and it is His will that there should precede it the extraordinary prayers of His people. *"I will yet for this be inquired of by the house of Israel, to do this for them."* (Ezekiel 36:37). In Zechariah 12:10 it is revealed that when God is about to accomplish great things for His church, He will begin by a remarkable pouring out of *"the Spirit of grace and supplication."* It is a spiritual law bound to the kingdom of heaven that blessings of great magnitude are not imparted except to prayers of the deepest urgency.

Prayer is our foundation from which we exercise and grow in the faith, which is essential in our witnessing. It is the finished work of Christ through the prompting power of the Holy Spirit that draws souls to the Savior in evangelism. Prayer is the power behind, in the mist of, and in front of faith (Ezekiel 36:24-32; John 3:5; 30; 20:21-23). To be effective in our service to Christ, we have to be a person who prays—and does so regularly. To witness, we must be praying for the soul of each person we encounter that day. When we witness we plant the seeds of life, but it is God who causes the growth (1 Cor. 3:6-7). In prayer you ask God to give that growth, to fulfill His promise. In prayer you ask God to convict the unrepentant of their sins and awaken in them the need for salvation. In prayer you *"let your requests be made known to God"* (Philippians 4:6).

Jesus specifically asked us to pray to the Father and ask Him to send workers into the field (Matt. 9:37-38). What is the field? It is the world of the unregenerate. Jesus wants people to find salvation and enter into eternal fellowship with Him. He has given the command *"Go therefore and make disciples of all the nations"* (Matt. 28:19). The Lord taught us the proper method of prayer in Luke 11:1-4, showing us that we need to be praying for workers, for ourselves, for opportunities, and for those who do not know Him. We need to pray and ask God to give us strength, love, and spiritual insight.

Implementing prayer in evangelism for the sake of reaping fruit necessitates the combined effort of all God's people, whatever their place or position in society and service in the Church. Those in positions of leadership are vested with God's authority to teach and lead the church in prayer for the reason of edification, purification and evangelism. They have a sobering responsibility to train, mentor and become the models for believers in prayer and evangelism. All Christians are evangelists, whereas we move among non-believers daily, uniquely Christ's "living epistles" to share the good news.

The Apostle Paul states in Eph. 6:12, *"For we do not wrestle against flesh and blood, but against the rulers, against*

[PRAYER ESSENTIAL FOR EVANGELISM]

the authorities, against the cosmic powers over this present darkness, against the spiritual forces of evil in the heavenly places." Not only must we contend with the strongholds that hold sinners captive, but there are also demonic forces at work in people's lives as well. Jesus said about Himself in relation to Satan in the Gospel of John 14:30, *"...the ruler of the world is coming, and he has nothing in Me."* There was nothing in Jesus that Satan could operate through, despite his best attempts in the desert. However, with us, demonic powers can subvert our minds by means of wayward thoughts and meditations. When we choose to believe something that is not true, these fallacious positions grant satanic powers access to our minds to work out devilish ambitions. Because we as Christians are aware of this frailty, we cry out daily as Paul did, *"Wretched man that I am; who will free me from the body of this death"* (Romans 7:24).

We are given promise by the Lord's words found in Luke 10:19, *"Behold, I have given you authority to tread on serpents and scorpions, and over all the power of the enemy, and nothing shall hurt you."* Jesus reveals to us in this passage that we as believers already have power over all the authority and power of Satan. Therefore before we go out on the field we need to pray and claim authority over these demonic forces that would try to impede the gospel from touching the hearts of those who would hear. Additionally, we need to pray also that these hindering spirits would be bound while we are witnessing so that their minds and hearts can respond to the gospel.

One of the enemy's schemes is to infiltrate the Church and compromise the power of prayer. Prayer then becomes self-focused rather than God-focused. Too often we call out for God's blessing and prosperity on our lives or voice any number of self-seeking ambitions without seeking God's purpose in our circumstances. Especially during economic or health trials, we may be tempted to pray for a restored life instead of a devoted one. Our prayers must shift from

[FINDING THE BALANCE IN WORLD MISSIONS]

"God, bless me" to "God, give me your heart. Help me to understand your purpose."

Pastor L. John Bueno, executive director of AG World Missions, wrote about prayer and missions from personal experience:

> By 1970, I had struggled for nine years pastoring a church in San Salvador, El Salvador, but the attendance couldn't seem to get above 300. I felt I had done everything humanly possible to make it grow. I had gone to every conference I could think of and studied a wide variety of strategies for church growth. Nothing seemed to work for me.
>
> I had no idea that God was about to bring an incredible breakthrough. A small group of young people came to me with a simple request: Could they start an all-night prayer meeting? They made plans to meet on Friday nights, and on the first Friday, 13 committed young men and women came to pray for our church. The group grew steadily. Soon, as many as 200 people were praying.
>
> To this day, when people ask me how the church grew from 100 to 22,000 and I say, "prayer," or "the lordship of Jesus Christ," I get the same response: "Tell us what really happened." People don't want to hear about prayer; that's too simple. They want to hear about a methodology they can copy. But I discovered just how empty methodologies can be. It's when Jesus Christ is truly exalted as Lord in His Church that the impossible quickly becomes possible.

Prayer is what enables us to recognize Jesus truly as Lord, the provider, the one who empowers all things. The great revivals and great churches of history reflect this principle. The 1860's Prayer Meeting Revival in the United States began with one faithful, praying man in New York City. Jeremiah Lanphier could hardly pronounce his own name without stuttering. But at his pastor's urging he started a prayer meeting in one of the upper rooms at his Dutch Reformed church in Manhattan as a lay missionary. At that time, drunkenness was rampant, and the nation was divided

[PRAYER ESSENTIAL FOR EVANGELISM]

by slavery. That small group grew into one of the greatest revivals our country has ever experienced.

Lanphier would begin each day going from office to office, house to house, and shop to shop, but by midday he was physically, emotionally and spiritually worn out. He discovered that, even as the body needs food, the soul and spirit need prayer. Lanphier realized his need and regularly returned to a room in the church Consistory building to cry out to God for spiritual strength. This fresh, personal experience of the power of prayer suggested to Lanphier that there might be others, especially those engaged in business, which might profit from time in prayer. He handed out some 20,000 flyers advertising the first noonday prayer meeting on September 23, 1857.

For the first thirty minutes he sat alone praying. Eventually, steps were heard coming up the staircase and another joined. Then another and another, until Lanphier was joined by five men. The next Wednesday the six increased to twenty. The following week there were 40. Lanphier and the others then decided to meet daily, and within weeks thousands of business leaders were meeting for prayer each day. Before long over 100 churches and public meeting halls were filled with noonday prayer meetings. God moved so powerfully that similar prayer meetings sprang up around the nation. For a season there were 10,000 conversions to Christ each week in New York City, and it is estimated that nearly one million people across the U.S. were transformed during this incredible move of God.

There are many other examples of praying saints who changed the face of Christendom. On May 15, 1958, a worship service was held in the home of Choi Ja-shil in Seoul, South Korea. Along with another pastor, David Yonggi Cho, Choi began a vigorous campaign of knocking on doors, providing spiritual help to the poor, and praying for the sick. Within their own ranks, they had dedicated prayer warriors on their knees daily; crying out for the Lord's will be done. Within months, the church had grown to fifty members. Worship services were moved to a tent pitched in the backyard. As the church continued to grow over the following months and years, it outgrew one tent after another. Yoido Full Gospel Church in Seoul, South Korea, is the world's largest church of 830,000 active members, grown in the power of prayer.

Prayer is a privilege and it is a powerful tool required in the work of the faithful witness. Without it you will be a foolish worker in the fields of the dead, those who can only be awakened spiritually. Pray and ask the Lord of the harvest to raise the dead to life through His power. Bend your knees in fellowship with your Lord. Prayer is where you meet Him. Prayer is where you are shaped.

"Prayer is the greatest power God has put into our hands for service—praying is harder than doing, at least I find it so, but the dynamic lays that way to advance the Kingdom." ~ Mary Slessor, Scottish missionary to Nigeria (1848-1915).

[17]
DIRECTION UNDER GOD'S SPIRIT

We understand that Christians are called to share the good news of Christ with all peoples and nations. A question that is rarely asked, should a Christian without constraint share the gospel without constraint wherever and whenever an opportunity arises? Scripture does say we should be ready in season and out of season to give an account of the faith that dwells within us. 1 Peter 3:15 reminds us *"...but in your hearts honor Christ the Lord as holy, always being prepared to make a defense to anyone who asks you for a reason for the hope that is in you."*

There is the commission that Christ gave as a command, combined with the Holy Spirit's guidance behind that directive, which could be classified as two distinctly separate, yet combined elements. We should not confuse compulsion of the flesh with specific direction from the Spirit. Philip was persuaded to share the gospel freely, but an angel gave him divine and distinct guidance to go to meet an Ethiopian in Acts 8:27. Philip could have traveled to a local town based on compulsion but chose instead to be guided by God's spiritual direction.

> "Now an angel of the Lord said to Philip, "Rise and go toward the south to the road that goes down from Jerusalem to Gaza." This is a desert place. And he rose and went. And there was an Ethiopian, a eunuch, a court official of Candace, queen of the Ethiopians, who was in charge of all her treasure. He had come to Jerusalem to worship and was returning, seated in his chariot, and he was reading the prophet Isaiah. And the Spirit said to Philip, "Go over and join this chariot." So Philip ran to him and heard him reading Isaiah the prophet and asked, "Do you understand what you are reading?" And he said, "How can

I, unless someone guides me?" And he invited Philip to come up and sit with him" (Acts 8:26-31).

One of the details that stand out in this story is that a very unlikely candidate for conversion to Christ is found and his heart's eyes opened through the supernatural leading of the Lord himself, and not through human planning. The person was from Ethiopia in Africa and had come all the way up to Jerusalem (at least 500 miles) to worship God (v. 27). Out of all the tens of thousands of Jews, Gentiles and Samaritans in the area that needed Christ, the Lord sovereignly sets His favor on this man and sends an angel to Philip, the deacon-evangelist, and instructs him to travel to a specific location.

Another example of Spirit-guided evangelism is that of Paul, who was persuaded to share the gospel in Asia and had the inner compulsion to do so, but the Holy Spirit forbade him and instead he traveled to Bithynia, and again, the Holy Spirit did not permit them to speak, so passing Mysia they came instead to Troas (Acts 16:6-8). To us logically, this does not make sense. Why give a command to share the gospel, only to have a spokesman to pass by potential hearers? Then we must remember, *"For my thoughts are not your thoughts, neither are your ways my ways, declares the Lord"* Isaiah 55:8. Do we seek God's guidance on matters of evangelism, or it is more consistent with random impulses or calculated methods, asking God to bless our ambitions?

It might seem inconsistent or a paradox that the Lord's global commission would command the faithful to go preach the gospel to the uttermost, only to prohibit speaking when there was an open opportunity. Paul was searching to see where God was at work and in the process it became evident the Holy Spirit was the one doing the forbidding. The holy Administrator of missions had closed the door. That is not where He was at work currently: *"...but the Spirit of Jesus did not allow them"* (v. 7b).

Note how God opens the doors in verses 9-10. They were now at Troas, near the site of ancient Troy. In verse 9, Luke,

[DIRECTION UNDER GOD'S SPIRIT]

the writer of Acts, tells us, *"A vision appeared to Paul in the night: a man of Macedonia was standing and appealing to him, and saying, 'Come over to Macedonia and help us.'"* Come, "help us" to obtain salvation. This is a Macedonian man pleading to hear the gospel.

God's Spirit is at work within all His children and He invites us to come and sacrificially join Him in His work of eternal redemption. What a shame when we move forward according to our own wisdom and in our own strength to fulfill our understanding of God's predestined will. (Sentence moved down) Verse 10 gives us the reasoned conclusion and consensus of the evangelists: *"When he had seen the vision, immediately we sought to go into Macedonia, concluding that God had called us to preach the gospel to them."* This passage reveals to us that God is already at work and He chooses to invite us to come and join Him under His distinct leadership and direction.

This was the clear direction that Paul needed. It was a group consensus. They sensed the same leading and approved the conclusion of Paul. The word "concluding" means "to make go together, to knit together." They came to the conclusion after looking at the evidence that this is where God wants them to go and work. God can use many different ways to guide and lead us.

We can observe the response of Paul and his companions, to the call of God. They acted on what they had received to be the will of God. The next day they went to the harbor, purchased their tickets and set sail by boat to the port city of Neapolis. They proceeded without deviation to the district of Macedonia. *"So putting out to sea from Troas, we ran a straight course to Samothrace, and on the day following to Neapolis; and from there to Philippi, which is a leading city of the district of Macedonia, a Roman colony; and we were staying in this city for some days"* (vv. 11-12).

The Holy Spirit led Paul to Philippi (v. 12), to a prayer meeting down by a riverside (v. 13). That location is where

God's hand was at work and the place He wanted His messengers to proclaim His message of sovereign grace. God will direct us to share the blessed news of Christ's redemptive plan of salvation where the hearts are receptive, where He is at work. God does not desire that we at random simply share the gospel on any street corner or at every door, but to seek His counsel through prayer and waiting on His leading. It is not enough to be a spiritual soldier with a command to go forth and serve, but we must be precisely and correctly led by the Holy Spirit.

Such governance is often lacking in the modern Church, where calculated methodologies has replaced waiting, listening, and seeking spiritual guidance. We should be often in counsel with God through prayer and attentive listening, so that we are aware when we should speak as prompted in every situation. This can be a challenge with systematic door-to-door cold calling and street corner evangelism, because if it is not distinctly guided by God it can be routinely initiated outside the guidance of the Holy Spirit, bearing little fruit.

A modern example of how the guidance of the Holy Spirit works is that of an Australian missionary who went with his family to Port Moresby, Papua New Guinea in 1970. He began a little church and was invited to preach in the northern province of Popondetta. He was taken to a village that had never heard the gospel and began to share the message of salvation. While he was speaking about Jesus, the Holy Spirit impressed upon him that a young woman in the village was deaf. He told the villagers what the Spirit had communicated to him and shared how the power of Christ can perform miracles and healings. Some of the women left the meeting and returned minutes later with a woman. They led the lady to the middle of the group and said, "This is the woman. She's deaf." While laying hands on her, the missionary prayed, "Lord Jesus, heal her right now," and the Lord did.

[DIRECTION UNDER GOD'S SPIRIT]

In that village there were four sorcerer brothers who had put a curse on this woman because she had offended them. What was being demonstrated through the Spirit's guidance was that the power of Jesus was greater than demonic power. The people witnessed this and the whole village believed. The four brothers committed their lives to the Lord and changed their allegiance from animism to faith in Christ. Like wildfire, the message of Christ spread into surrounding villages. Thirty-six years later, there are over five hundred churches and fifteen Bible schools, all run by Papua New Guineans, and missionaries in Vanuatu, the Solomon Islands, Fiji, the Philippines, India and Australia.

The Holy Spirit beckons men and women who look and watch and wait and follow. G. Campbell Morgan captures the heart of the great passage found in Acts in his application:

> The Spirit guided by the vision of the man of Macedonia. Here is the revelation of the fact that the Spirit guides, not by flaming visions always, not by words articulate in human ears; but by circumstances, by commonplace things, by difficult things, by dark things, by disappointing things. The Spirit guides, molds and fashions the entire pathway.

When Jesus was alive on earth and guided His disciples, He was not only filled with the Spirit, He was God: *"I and the Father are one"* (John 10:30). As the Godhead, He instructed them not to go to the Gentiles to preach (Matt. 15:24). His sending out of the disciples preceded the coming of the Holy Spirit that would personally guide each believer. Jesus as God provided direction about whom, when and where to go, not at all sporadic or uncalculated evangelism as we sometimes are persuaded to do.

In John 14:26 we read, *"But the Helper, the Holy Spirit, whom the Father will send in my name, he will teach you all things and bring to your remembrance all that I have said to you."* Again in John 16:13, it says that *"When the Spirit of truth comes, he will guide you into all the truth, for he will not speak on his own authority, but whatever he hears he will speak, and he will declare to you the things that are to come."* The Holy Spirit would be as a guide, He goes before, leads the way, removes obstructions, opens the understanding, makes things plain and clear, teaches the way people should go. To be led into a truth is more than barely to know it; it is not only to have the notion of it in our heads, but power of it in our hearts. He shall teach all truth, and keep back nothing profitable, for he will show things to come.

"Not speaking of himself; speaking what he hears" tell us the Holy Spirit is the passive receiver of divine information which he then relates to those He inhabits. The source of the information which the Spirit hears and speaks must be either Jesus or the Father who speaks to the Spirit who then relays the message to believers. In either case, the Spirit is not deemed to be the originator of the words but a translating agent of either Jesus or the Father. This phrase, *"He shall not speak of himself,"* is a common Johanine phrase, most often applied to Jesus Christ as a sort of hallmark of His ministry. It was Jesus who, while on earth, did "not speak of himself," who in all things that He spoke attributed His words to an enabler, to the Father, who enabled Him to speak in power and gave Him the words with prevailing authority.

John 16:13 inevitably refers to the inhabiting Spirit of the exalted Christ. Jesus continues to possess His divine capacities even while He inhabits believers. He operates within a believer through the Spirit in relation to God who is the sustainer of humanity. He continues to speak as He spoke on earth, as a prophet and mouthpiece of God. Through his cohabitation, He will guide us too, if we are willing.

God states in his Word, *"I will instruct you and teach you in the way you should go; I will counsel you and watch over you. Do not be like the horse or the mule, which have no understanding but must be controlled by bit and bridle"* (Psalm 32:8-9). Horses and mules need to be forcibly controlled. These animals are excusable, since they "have

[Direction Under God's Spirit]

no understanding "or "no discernment." Israel would be inexcusable, since it had the gift of reason as do Christians under the covenant of grace. We must not be ill-natured and mischievous as not only hating instruction, but kicking and spurning at, persecuting those who might be sent by God to share revelations that might contest our own understandings.

Not everything kingdom-related is subject to distinct direction. As one matures in the faith, the Lord will allow more self-governance under His leading. Take, for instance, Hudson Taylor who founded the China Inland Mission. In his younger days as a Christian, God's direction used to come to him very clearly. The Lord would often guide him in very specific ways. "But," he said, "Now as I have gone on, and God has used me more and more, I seem often to be like a man going along in a fog. I do not know what to do." In his later years, when he was responsible for the leadership of a thousand missionaries in China, he often found guidance more difficult. Why? Simply because, being as mature as he was in his knowledge of the Scriptures and the ways of God, the Lord trusted him to make the right decisions without step by step directions.

This is a mark of maturity. As a good frame of reference, when our children are small we have to tell them what is right and wrong, instruct them to go here or to go there. If they have been trained well, then they will be able in maturity to make their own right decisions. Eugene H. Peterson, Professor Emeritus of Spiritual Theology at Regent College, explains this well. He writes:

> The early stages of Christian belief are not infrequently marked with miraculous signs and exhilarations of spirit. But as discipleship continues the sensible comforts (those that depend on our physical senses) gradually disappear, for God does not want us neurotically dependent upon him, but willingly trustful in him. And so he weans us.

A good analogy is provided by Peter's deliverance from prison in Acts, chapter twelve. The angel comes to Peter and wakes him up. His chains fall off. We could liken this to conversion when we awake spiritually, and the power of those things that bind us and keep us from being what God intended are broken. Peter then follows the angel with no understanding as to how he is to get out of the prison, or where he is going. In fact, initially he thinks he is dreaming. However, when he reaches the door of the cell, it opens. He keeps following, and when he reaches the end of the corridor, the next door opens. There is still the massive gate of the prison. However, when they come to it, it too opens. The point we want to comprehend is, the doors of God do not open till we reach them.

God wants us to trust him to open the right doors at the right time. And if we arrive at a door and it doesn't open, it could be that God is prompting us to wait as until we have matured in certain areas first. Sometimes it is a matter of Him turning us in another direction. However, we mustn't gaze so longingly at one door that might be closed that we miss the one that has been open. It is okay to rattle a handle in prayer, but we must not try to force ourselves through. We must wait on the direction of the Spirit.

Paul wrote in 1 Cor. 2:1-3 about what it is that should guide our witness: *"And I, when I came to you, brothers, did not come proclaiming to you the testimony of God with lofty speech or wisdom. For I decided to know nothing among you except Jesus Christ and Him crucified."* Jesus guides it! We must know nothing but Jesus and His being poured out for all of humanity's sins. Everything else follows naturally in the Spirit and the Lord invites the rest of us to join in doing the same.

[18]
Suffering & Persecutions

In a society led by consumerism, the Church has been seduced by modernistic ideologies which effect Christian missiology as well. Affluent cultures are intrinsically built on the effort to escape suffering and pain while seeking to be encompassed by pleasure and luxuries. Can it be that in the preoccupation with the good life in progressive nations, we have overlooked the biblical principle of suffering woven all throughout the New Testament?

If Jesus suffered, why do we treat suffering with such alarm and confusion? The Greeks and the Jews in Paul's day scoffed at the Christian teaching on suffering and weakness. Many authors over the years have commented on how the western Church in general is infatuated with efficiency and productivity which in its worldly tenor, is at odds with the biblical portrait that portrays a "theology of suffering." The well-known German pastor and theologian Helmut Thielicke commented that the inability to translate the gospel into our culture today can be seen best in the avoidance of embracing the biblical teaching on suffering.

One passage in Phil. 1:29-30 reveals to us that suffering for the Lord Jesus is a basic part of discipleship and is to be expected and even embraced. Kenneth S. Wuest's **Word Studies from the Greek New Testament** translates this passage to read, *"And the reason why you should not be terrified is because to you that very thing was given graciously as a favor for the sake of Christ and in His behalf, not only to be believing on Him but also to be suffering for His sake and in His behalf."*

From the *Exposition of Philippians* by Charles H. Spurgeon, he comments further on this passage,

"What an honor this is to be conferred upon any follower of Christ,—"not only to believe on him, but also to suffer for his sake"! It is not every Christian who receives this mark of honor. There are some believers who have peculiarly tender places in their hearts, and who are wounded and gashed by the unkind remarks of those who love them not because they love the Lord Jesus Christ. To you, my brother, my sister, it is given—and you may well rejoice in such a gift,—"not only to believe on him, but also to suffer for his sake."

The apostle Paul was in his final imprisonment, awaiting execution. The ever so meek Timothy was not convinced that he wanted to follow in the apostle's footsteps if it meant imprisonment and martyrdom. He may have been wondering if there might be a little safer, more pleasant line of work to get into. Paul pleads with him not to be ashamed of the gospel or of Paul, the prisoner, but to join with him in suffering for the gospel. Paul mentions this in every chapter of this letter. In 2 Tim. 2:3 he writes, *"Suffer hardship with me, as a good soldier of Christ Jesus."* In 3:12, he re-emphasizes, *"Indeed, all who desire to live godly in Christ Jesus will be persecuted."* Again in verses 4:5 he exhorts Timothy to "endure hardship" in his ministry.

"Therefore" in 2 Tim. 1:8 points us back to 1:5-7: *"Because you are saved, Timothy, and God has given you a spiritual gift to use in serving Him, therefore, join with me in suffering for the gospel."* Paul is making the point. When you serve Christ, be prepared to suffer for the gospel. You must accept the reality of suffering as part of the journey.

In Matt. 13:44, Jesus shared the parable of the man who found a treasure hidden in a field. From rejoicing over it, he went and sold all that he had to buy that field. Christ indicated that the gospel about life in Him is that treasure. He told a similar parable in Matt. 13:45-46, about the merchant who found a pearl of great value and he sold all that he had to buy it. Jesus and the gospel are that pearl of great price. If we have found eternal life in Him, we have

[SUFFERING AND PERSECUTIONS]

everything that we need for time and eternity, regardless of the suffering entailed.

The Bible as a whole shows us that serving God engages us in combat with the devil, and that God does not promise to keep us from suffering in the midst of the battle. Jesus sent out the disciples as sheep among wolves, warning that they would be persecuted because of the gospel (Matt. 10:16-17; Luke 21:12-19). Paul wrote in Romans 8:35-36, *"Who will separate us from the love of Christ? Will tribulation, or distress, or persecution, or famine, or nakedness, or peril, or sword? Just as it is written, 'For Your sake we are being put to death all day long; we were considered as sheep to be slaughtered.'"* The implication is that God's people have to endure all manner of perilous trials.

Hebrews 11:35b-38 reflects upon the men of faith who:

"...were tortured, refusing to accept release, so that they might rise again to a better life. Others suffered mocking and flogging, and even chains and imprisonment. They were stoned, they were sawn in two, and they were killed with the sword. They went about in skins of sheep and goats, destitute, afflicted, mistreated—of whom the world was not worthy—wandering about in deserts and mountains, and in dens and caves of the earth."

Where does modern Christianity come up with the idea that if we dedicate our lives to Jesus Christ, He will spare us from suffering and hardship? Without clear direction from biblical insight, we might think of missions, *"It will be a great adventure and equally fulfilling to serve the Lord."* Instead, the Lord instructs us in Luke 14:28-33 to sit down and first consider the cost based on the facts. You're being deployed into enemy territory. There will be attacks and setbacks and even friendly fire from your own troops. Anyone in service to the Lord must accept the reality of suffering before we commit to serving Him at any capacity.

Paul was chained in a dark Roman dungeon, being criticized and attacked, even by his fellow Christians. Almost everyone had abandoned this faithful apostle who was poured out for God in Jesus. How could he retain any hope in this difficult situation? One of the key comments made by Paul was, "me His prisoner." Surely it was Caesar's officials that had arrested Paul, making him Caesar's prisoner? From Paul's perspective, he was the prisoner of the Lord, the King of kings, the sovereign of the universe. One way to endure any criticism or suffering that you encounter while serving the Lord is to remember that He is sovereign over everything. Do we have faith that God has a purpose in allowing His faithful to endure hardships and sufferings?

"Do not be ashamed of the testimony of our Lord...." The testimony of our Lord is the message of the Savior who died on a Roman cross in shame. Although the Jews did not practice crucifixion, sometimes they would hang a dead body on a stake or a tree as a public object lesson of shame (Joshua 10:26; 1 Samuel 31:10; 2 Samuel 21:1-9). They considered such men accursed by God (Deut. 21:22-23; Gal. 3:13). Paul wrote in 1 Cor. 1:18, *"For the word of the cross is foolishness to those who are perishing."* A few verses later (1:22-23) he adds, *"For indeed Jews ask for signs and Greeks search for wisdom; but we preach Christ crucified, to Jews a stumbling block and to Gentiles foolishness..."*

From the Introduction to **Filling Up the Afflictions of Christ** by Pastor John Piper, we can read his meaningful and noteworthy insights:

> More and more I am persuaded from Scripture and from the history of missions that God's design for the evangelization of the world and the consummation of his purposes includes the suffering of his ministers and missionaries. To put it more plainly and specifically, God designs that the suffering of his ambassadors is one essential means in the triumphant spread of the good news among all the peoples of the world.
>
> I am saying more than the obvious fact that suffering is a result of faithful obedience in spreading the gospel. That is true. Jesus said suffering will result from this faithfulness. *"You will*

[SUFFERING AND PERSECUTIONS]

be hated by all for my name's sake" (Luke 21:17). *"If they persecuted me, they will also persecute you"* (John 15:20). I am saying that this suffering is part of God's strategy for making known to the world who Christ is, how he loves, and how much he is worth.

This is both frightening and encouraging. It frightens us because we know that we may very likely be called to suffer in some way in order to get the breakthrough we long to see in a hard frontline mission's situation. But it also encourages us because we can know that our suffering is not in vain and that the very pain that tends to dishearten us is the path to triumph, even when we can't see it.

Pastor Piper comments further saying that if we are faithful to God's command to take the gospel to the remaining unreached peoples, some of the leaders and some families will be sacrificed in the process. This is by God's design, as the Bible and Church history repeatedly demonstrate. In fact, God has predetermined a specific number of martyrs (see Rev. 6:10-11). Matthew Henry's Concise Commentary expounds with clarity upon this passage in Revelations:

> God has provided a good place in the better world, for those who are faithful unto death. It is not their own death, but the sacrifice of Christ, that gives them entrance into heaven. The cause in which they suffered, was for the word of God; the best any man can lay down his life for; faith in God's word, and the unshaken confession of that faith. They commit their cause to Him to whom vengeance belongs. The Lord is the comforter of his afflicted servants, and precious is their blood in his sight. As the measure of the sin of persecutors is filling up, so is the number of the persecuted, martyred servants of Christ. When this is fulfilled, God will send tribulation to those who trouble them, and unbroken happiness and rest to those that are troubled.

The postmodern seeker-sensitive church markets the gospel by making the message more palatable to unbelievers and believers, as a socially beneficial and positive moral choice.

[Finding the Balance in World Missions]

They reduce or sometimes remove sin and judgment which are offensive among their target audiences. This "other gospel" assertively promotes how Jesus can help all those who come to Him reach their full potential, or how He can give you a fulfilling life largely protected from undesirable discomforts. This is a false gospel.

Regardless, the divinely authored gospel is not about helping us fulfill our dreams for happiness and success during our lifetimes. The testimony of our Lord is the assurance of a crucified Savior. He died to rescue sinners from the awful eternal judgment that we deserve. While such a message will not "sell" in today's self-focused culture, it is the only message the divinely inspired gospel unveils.

Pastor John MacArthur at one point mused that God couldn't have created a more unworldly way to market the gospel than by a crucified Savior. However, if you disregard or minimize the cross to make the gospel (Church) more marketable, you eliminate the gospel. The simple and essential message of the crucified Savior is as powerful to convert an intellectual at the university as it is to save a tribesman in the jungle. Instead of being ashamed of the cross, Paul gloried in it (Gal. 6:14). Paul was calling Timothy (and us) not to be ashamed of the testimony of our Lord, which is the message of the cross. Proclaim it without compromise despite any earthly peril or rejection.

Adoniram Judson, who suffered incredible trials in taking the gospel to Burma, said, "If I had not felt certain that every additional trial was ordered by infinite love and mercy, I would not have survived my accumulated sufferings" quoted from ***Adoniram Judson's Life Text*** by F.W. Boreham.

Born in 1788, and converted in his early twenties, Judson and his bride Ann sailed in 1812 with a group of the first missionaries to go out from American soil. After a difficult four-month voyage, they arrived in India only to hear very discouraging reports about Burma, in addition learning that they could not stay in India. They spent the next year sailing

[SUFFERING AND PERSECUTIONS]

from India to Mauritius (off the coast of South Africa) and back, to avoid deportation.

They finally arrived in Rangoon, Burma, a horrendously dirty, fly-infested town, and began the arduous task of learning Burmese. They found the Burmese people to be committed to Buddhism and not at all interested in and opposed to Christianity. They were the only English-speaking couple in Rangoon, therefore the Judson's were isolated as they struggled with the language and the mission. The birth of a son brightened their lives, but at eight months, he grew desperately sick. With no doctors or medicine in Rangoon, the baby died. They buried him next to their home and continued with the Lord's work through their tears.

After six years of unfruitful toil, they finally baptized their first Burmese convert. A handful more came forward over the next few years. Then, in 1824, the British went to war against the Burmese. The Judson's were in the capital city, Ava, and Adoniram was imprisoned, falsely accused of being a British spy. When they arrested a man, they slipped a small, hard cord behind the back and around a man's arms, just above the elbow. They could yank this cord so tight that it often dislocated the arms, sometimes cutting off the breath, and could even make blood spurt from the nose and mouth of the prisoner. After hauling Judson to the prison, they secured his feet with three sets of iron fetters that cut into his ankles.

The prison was a sweltering bamboo room, with an overwhelming stench. There were no windows, but a little light filtered through the cracks in the wall. At night, the prison warden would come in with an assistant. They would slide a long bamboo pole through the fetters on each man's legs and hoisted it up with a block and tackle until only the prisoner's shoulders and heads rested on the floor. They left them suspended in this position all night, while the rats ran around them. Ann was pregnant and had to walk two miles each way to bring Adoniram food each day. After 17 months of torture, including a move to a farther location, where he had to walk barefoot over sharp, hot rocks and nearly died, Judson was released.

This is only a glimpse of the hardships that he and family had to endure over the years. On April 12, 1850 Adoniram Judson went home to be with his Savior, to experience God's love first hand. At the time of his death there were 63 churches and 7,000 converts as a result of his commitment. Today in Burma (Myanmar), according to Operation World (Patrick Johnstone & Jason Mandryk, 21st Century Edition, p. 462), there are over 3,700 Baptist churches with a total membership of over 600,000, plus many other evangelical churches. The Burmese church today, although under frequent persecution, sends out many missionaries under their own resources. Suffering was a devout man's price to serve the Lord, but the Kingdom work was enlarged greatly.

"He is no fool who gives up what he cannot keep to gain that which he cannot lose." ~ Jim Elliot, missionary martyr who lost his life in the late 1950's trying to reach the Auca Indians of Ecuador.

[19]
SCRIPTURAL BENEVOLENCE IN MISSION

A question that sometimes arises is one that challenges the benevolence of the believer, *"Is it scriptural for a church or organization to give money to people who are in need who are not Christians?"* It is difficult to arrive at a single conclusion, where any number of variables might present an exception. But there are some general guidelines reflected in Scripture, which may surprise many of us who already have a position based on traditional or denominational persuasions. Due to the confusion related to this subject, readers will find this chapter heavily annotated with scriptural references.

In the Old Testament, we can read that God clarifies to the Israelites that they are to care for widows, orphans, immigrants and the poor (Zech. 7:10-11). And it is in Micah 6:8 that they are exhorted to "do justice and love mercy." While the words justice and mercy may sound different, they are not. The Hebrew word for mercy is *chesedh*: God's unconditional grace and compassion for us. In essences, it means God will never withdraw his support from us where His infinite wisdom and love are always present on our behalf. The Hebrew word for justice is *mishpat*, which occurs more than 200 times in the Old Testament. It emphasizes action, and means treating people equitably and caring for those who can't care for themselves. To walk with God, then, we must do justice out of merciful love or in another words, we must take action with a loving attitude.

The Canon of Scripture repeatedly emphasizes the need for Christians to care for the poor as one of the fundamental actions synonymous with the gospel message. Jesus himself was born to poor parents (cf. Luke 2:24 and note) and had few possessions during his public ministry (Matt. 8:20).

Jesus says that as his followers do, or do not do, to *"the least of these"* (i.e. those who are hungry, thirsty, strangers, naked), so they either do it, or do not do it, to him (cf. Matt. 25:35-45. Also see Prov. 14:31, 19:17, 21:13).

Paul and the early Church took Jesus' teaching seriously and were eager *"to remember the poor"* (Gal. 2:10). In fact, Paul anchored his appeal to care for the poor in Jerusalem by means of Jesus' own atoning self-sacrifice: *"though he was rich, yet for your sake he became poor"* (2 Cor. 8:9). The generosity of the church both within and outside the family of faith eventually led the anti-Christian 'Julian the Apostate' who was a Roman Emperor from 361 to 363 AD, a noted philosopher and Greek writer, to complain: *"Nothing has contributed to the progress of the superstition of the Christians as their charity to strangers...The impious Galileans provide not only for their own poor, but for ours as well"* (Julian, Epistles 84). The care of the poor referenced often takes the form of meeting immediate needs for food, clothing, and other essentials (cf. Luke 10:25-36; James 2:15-17; 1 John 3:17-18).

There is no question that individual Christians, according to their ability, were commanded to provide benevolence in the manner of deeds and tangible resources for unbelievers. In James 1:27, the writer admonished the believers to *"visit the fatherless and widows in the affliction..."* Also, in Galatians 6:10, Paul told the brethren to *"do good to all men, especially the household of faith."* In context, neither of these passages were commands for church or organizational action since all the related commands in the adjoining text can only be fulfilled by individual action.

Paul faced many of these same benevolence challenges in his own day. Although he did not request personal support, he spent close to ten years soliciting funds for what is commonly referred to as the "Jerusalem collection." This was a collection he took up among the Gentile churches to help Judean believers who were facing a difficult economic crisis as a result of a famine during the mid to late 40's A.D. Paul and Barnabas made an initial famine-relief visit to Jerusalem in A.D. 46 and delivered a monetary gift from the church at Antioch (Acts 11:29-30). At that time the Jerusalem church expressed hope that the believers with Paul would continue to remember the Judean believers, which Paul was more than eager to do (Gal. 2:10).

The collection effort was successfully completed in A.D. 57, and the funds were delivered by Paul and a group of delegates chosen by the contributing Gentile churches. In Romans 15:26 Paul states that the churches of Macedonia and Achaia *"were pleased to make a contribution for the poor among the saints in Jerusalem,"* but the actual list of contributing churches is much longer. Luke's list includes delegates from Berea, Thessalonica, Derbe and Asia. The church at Philippi is without a delegate, but Luke himself may have functioned in this capacity considering the "we" mention in Acts. Timothy, who is included in the list, undoubtedly represented Lystra. Corinth was also without a delegate, but they may well, in the end, have asked Paul or possibly Titus to represent them.

Two chapters of 2 Corinthians are devoted to the matter of the Jerusalem relief fund. The length attests to the seriousness with which the collection effort was viewed. According to 2 Cor. 8:10, Corinth was not only the first church to give but the only one that had a desire to do so. Paul must have made the Corinthians aware of the relief fund on his founding visit or shortly thereafter, for a little over a year later the church asked for his counsel on the best way to go about saving up donations (1 Cor. 16:1). His advice at the time was to do as he had instructed the Galatian churches: each person should set aside a sum of money every week in keeping with his or her income. In this way no collections would have to be organized on Paul's return visit (cf. 1 Cor. 16:2). The assumption that each person could do this shows that most members had surplus income. But it must not have been a very great surplus, since week-by-week savings were necessary for the contribution to be a generous one in the end (cf. 1 Cor. 16:2 and 2 Cor. 8:20).

As a subject of study, we can learn about how the early Church shared with one another primarily. When Paul collected money for the famine in Judea, we are not told that he was collecting money on behalf of those outside the Church, but rather those within. In addition, some spiritual leaders conclude that the Church should offer spiritual truth to the unregenerate prior to offering material sustenance. They teach that our calling is primarily to preach the gospel, not to feed the poor who will always be with us (cf. John 12:8). They conclude that our resources should be saved for evangelism instead.

This approach alone is obviously problematic. Jesus came preaching not only spiritual salvation but also freedom from social oppression (Luke 4:18-20). The two go hand in hand. When Jesus asked us to give to the poor, he did not specify the Christian poor only. On the contrary, Jesus told us to share without asking questions (Matt. 5:42). He also commanded us to be all-inclusive in our love (Matt. 5:43-48). Hence our giving is not to be limited to Christians only.

However, there is a priority to benevolence. Looking again at Galatians 6:10, Paul confirms this principle. He writes, *"So then, as we have opportunity, let us do good to everyone, and especially to those who are of the household of faith."* Note that the family comes first, then those who are not part of the family; thus charity is ultimately to be spread among all people, not believers only. As God was not tightfisted with us, neither are we to be penurious with others.

The Scriptures do mention of helping in a regular way those who have no way of working or providing for themselves. We see in Acts 6:1-7 the church appointed a group of people to help the widows of the church. The Bible references the kinds of people that have no way of working or providing for themselves which include widows and orphans (James

1:27). We have additional categories like single mothers to whom the church should give special attention. The church should help if the family cannot, but it should be the family's responsibility first to care for their own (1 Tim. 5:16).

The Scriptures also speak of helping those who are poor or suffering because of an emergency situation. We have already discussed Acts 11:28-30 which mentioned the famine in Judea where other church members collected funds to help those in need. The Bible instructs repeatedly to remember the poor, and not to turn away from those in need. Jesus placed such an emphasis on giving to the poor that he called those who lacked compassion, unbelievers (1 Tim. 5:8). Proverbs 21:13 is among the most powerful calls from God to help those who are hungry because *"If a man shuts his ears to the cry of the poor, he too will cry out and not be answered."*

James 2:15-17 and Gal. 6:10 both talk about the importance of caring for those inside the church. *"So then, as we have opportunity, let us do good to everyone, and especially to those who are of the household of faith."* We don't ignore those outside of the church, but we give priority to the needs of those in the family of God, as order of first importance.

The principle of tithing as revealed in the Old Testament was also to benefit those in need who were not part of the children of promise, those who dwelled within the gates of a town. In Deut. 14:27-29 we read, *"Also you shall not neglect the Levite who is in your town, for he has no portion or inheritance among you. At the end of every third year you shall bring out all the tithe of your produce in that year, and shall deposit it in your town. The Levite, because he has no portion or inheritance among you, and the alien, the orphan and the widow who are in your town, shall come and eat and be satisfied, in order that the LORD your God may bless you in all the work of your hand which you do."* We can quickly identify that the Lord considers those who are not citizens of the Kingdom as those equally worthy of our benevolence. Being blessed was dependent on this understanding.

[FINDING THE BALANCE IN WORLD MISSIONS]

We need to take a look at the collective action by a local church, after the New Covenant came into action starting with the book of Acts. In Acts 2:44-45 and 4:32-35 we note that during a time of great need it was believers who had all things common and were *"distributing to each as anyone had need."* Could this possibly have included unbelievers? In Acts 3:6, we have a lame man begging alms from Peter and John. Though we know that Peter and John with the other apostles had control of the money that was being collected by the Church for the believers (4:35, 37), Peter said, *"Silver and gold I do not have, but what I have, I give you...rise up and walk."* Peter is indirectly claiming not to have any personal money or resources that he could offer this unbeliever. What about the collected money from the local church bodies?

Later, in 1 Cor. 16:1-2, when Paul commanded the church in Corinth to take up collections on the first day of the week, he said, *"Now concerning the collection for the saints..."* Every time a church gave money for the purpose of benevolence in the New Testament, the passage had some reference to "the saints." Consider these additional passages: Acts 11:29; Rom. 15:25-27; II Cor. 8:1-4; I Tim. 5:3-16. From these, Paul additionally admonishes that a needy believer is not to be supported by the church if he has family who can provide for him or her first.

We should note that the first century believers set a high standard for giving. They sold their goods and gave money to any believer in need (Acts 2:45). They sold their property and gave the entire amount to the work of the apostles (Acts 4:36-5:2). And they also gave generously to the ministry of Paul (2 Cor. 8:1-5) on a continual basis (Phil. 4:16-18). From all these examples, tithing was for empowering the gospel of Christ and assisting the poor in the church. Paul also makes it clear that Christians are not to give *"grudgingly or under compulsion"* but as each believer has *"purposed in his heart"* (2 Cor. 9:7), and this is true for any church or organization as well. There is nothing objectionable about giving a freewill offering when the Spirit has moved us to aid a particular need or project. However, overall we should have a prayed over purpose and a plan to our giving.

One of the greater challenges in the Western church is the high standard of living with little consideration of others outside the immediate social circle. When comfortable, it is easy to neglect the commands of Jesus who says we are to love our neighbor as our self by evidence of action. When asked who is my neighbor Jesus told the story of the Good Samaritan who helped a *"stranger"*. As the Church is made up of followers of Christ we should follow his teaching with regards to strangers who may be poor, as did the early church and the world took notice.

In summation, we know that the Scriptures do not clarify every detail as we might like, but they do give us relatively clear instructions on where (or to whom) we should give. We should give to the poor and oppressed—especially within the Christian community (1 John 3:16-17). God has a special concern for the poor, specifically widows and orphans (Deut. 10:18-19; James 1:27), the hungry, the thirsty, the sick, the naked, aliens and prisoners (Matt. 25:34-40), as well as victims of calamity (Luke 10:30-37; Acts 11:27-30). Because the Christian community is our spiritual family, we are especially responsible for the Christian needy (Rom. 12:13), in the same way that we give special attention to our own spouses, children and parents before others (1 Tim. 5:8). Beyond this, we should give to the poor and needy in general, Christian or not (Deuteronomy 15:11).

We should also give to those who serve among us. Specifically, we should give to support pastors who care for us (1 Cor. 9:7-14; 1 Tim. 5:17-18) and to support missionaries (Phil. 4:15-19). We should give to the needs of our immediate family members (cf. 1 Tim. 5:4, 8, 16) though not in extravagant ways that sacrifices our ability to help the larger Christian family (1 Tim. 6:6-8). We should give what we owe to civil authorities, even if we believe we are being taxed unfairly. God has ordained civil authorities—imperfect as they may be—to oversee His work, and we are to financially empower them to do their jobs (Rom. 13:6-7). We should give to our enemies. This is perhaps a special mark of Christian generosity. Because God in Christ gave to us when we were His enemies, he calls us to be like him by giving to those who do not like or oppose us. This is the point of Jesus' story of the Good Samaritan (Luke 10:30-37) and of the Apostle Paul's instruction in Romans 12:20.

There are some passages that are parabolical; as the separating between the sheep and the goats, and the dialogues between the judge and the persons judged: but there is no thread of comparison carried through this discourse, rather it might be called a delineation of the final judgment. Jesus gave His listeners a startling wake-up call, describing those who would profess their belief in Him yet have not action to prove their confession.

> *"Then he will say to those on his left, 'Depart from me, you who are cursed, into the eternal fire prepared for the devil and his angels. For I was hungry and you gave me nothing to eat, I was thirsty and you gave me nothing to drink, I was a stranger and you did not invite me in, I needed clothes and you did not clothe me, I was sick and in prison and you did not look after me.' They also will answer, 'Lord, when did we see you hungry or thirsty or a stranger or needing clothes or sick or in prison, and did not help you?' He will reply, 'I tell you the truth, whatever you did not do for one of the least among you, you did not do for me'"* (Matt. 25:41-45).

[20]
THE INDIGENOUS CHURCH

The remaining chapters of this book are compiled more to assist with the mechanics of indigenous missions. While the content is geared more to those directly involved in missions, the lay reader will glean valued information and insight. We encourage you to continue on this journey.

An indigenous church is a church that is native to its surroundings. While the word "church" denotes a divine nature with regard to its character and unity, the word "indigenous" denotes a human cultural component, reflecting the "cultural milieu in which [the church] is planted," writes Paul A. Pomerville in his book *Introduction to Missions: An Independent-Study Textbook*. God uses the indigenous church to reach His creation. While being a church, the indigenous church has some unique characteristics that some churches do not have. It is a church that is adaptive to the particular culture of the people surrounding it.

Indigenous churches are churches suited to local culture and led by local Christians reared in their own culture. There have been two main strategies proposed for the creation of indigenous churches:

1. Where foreign missionaries create well-organized churches and then hand them over to local converts. The foreign mission is generally seen as temporary scaffolding which must be removed once the fellowship of believers is functioning properly. Missionaries provide teaching, pastoral care, buildings, finance and authority, and train local converts to take over these responsibilities. Thus, the church becomes indigenous. It becomes self-supporting, self-propagating and self-governing.

2. Where foreign missionaries do not create churches but instead help local converts develop their own spiritual gifts and leadership abilities and gradually develop their own churches. Missionaries then would provide teaching and pastoral care alone. The church is thus indigenous from the start. It will have always been self-supporting, self-propagating and self-governing.

It is not easy to plant a church in a distant country, guiding it to make a transition toward autonomy, but God has shown in His revealed Word that He will equip His people to accomplish the task. Melvin L. Hodges, in his book *The Indigenous Church*, states that "the three basic elements which make the church indigenous are: self-propagation, self-support, and self-government. Should any one of these essential elements be missing, the church is not truly indigenous."

The three basic elements shared below were an inspiration for William Taylor (1821–1902) who was an American Missionary Bishop of the Methodist Episcopal Church. However, it was in the 19th century that Rufus Anderson and Henry Venn developed the Three-Self Formula as criteria that would measure whether a church was indigenous.

1. **An indigenous church is self-governing.** While there needs to be a period of time where the foreign missionary governs the affairs of the newly established church, they must relinquish this control and appoint/train responsible local individuals to provide the church leadership, preaching, and teaching. Eph. 4:11-12 tells us that God *"gave the apostles, the prophets, the evangelists, the shepherds and teachers, to equip the saints for the work of ministry, for building up the body of Christ."* God will bestow upon native Christians the gifts necessary to administer and govern the church (1 Cor. 12; Rom. 12). The missionary must recognize the gifts from God in the local people and elect a pastor chosen along with elders. If the church is young and

lacking in spiritually mature men, a temporary board should be chosen to perform the duties of the office of a deacon.
2. **The indigenous church is self-supporting.** "The idea of self-support finds biblical basis in the church's stewardship and its dependence on God to meet all its needs" (Pomerville p. 190). Supporting Scriptures include Matt. 6:25-34; 2 Cor. 8:9; Phil. 4:10-19. While a missionary will probably begin the church with funds from his or her support organization, the indigenous people must not depend on this money, but must learn to depend on God to provide through their own local resources. Hodges writes "under ordinary circumstances even the poorest can support a pastor according to their own standard of living if there are ten or more faithful tithing families in the congregation" (p. 77). When the indigenous nationals contribute and sacrifice for their church, they will feel that they are a real part of its growth instead of being apathetic towards its needs.
3. **The indigenous church is self-propagating.** When the local people accept Christ, there is often a tremendous zeal that can be utilized toward evangelizing others. A properly trained national missionary will encourage and direct a new convert instead of stifling him or her. With the biblical emphasis on all members witnessing, and in time developing new converts in order for them to do the same, the church will be self-propagating without the ongoing efforts of a foreign missionary.

These three ideological concepts came to be known or referred to as the "indigenous church" concept. Later it was added the "4th self"—Self-theologizing. These assumptions were later widely challenged. A church can have all these qualities without being indigenous, and a church can be indigenous without having these three qualities. While this is true, these points still represent the fundamental framework for an indigenous church. Another insight into this formula that has merit comes from the book ***Planning Strategies for World Evangelization*** by Edward R. Dayton and David Allen Fraser:

> ...this formula (3-self's) is applicable only where the church grows rapidly. In resistant populations where individuals come to Christ slowly and only a few at a time, it is impossible to aim at a three-self church. Churches will not be large enough to carry out these principles or support auxiliary structures.... Furthermore, the three-self's do not invariable lead to increased rates of church growth. Some large churches have grown up on the basis of paid pastors and evangelists managed by foreigners. It is true that over time they moved in the direction of the three-self's. But their beginning and expansion were not due to following three-self principles.

Today, indigenous church theory moves beyond the three-self's understanding to suggest that mission churches must appropriately reflect their culture. Continued study on the subject reveals that not all church plants are genuinely indigenous. Hodges states in his book that "A church that must depend on foreigners for its workers that must call for additional missionaries to extend the work that must plead for foreign funds in order to keep going is not an indigenous church." He rebukes those leaders who do not have an indigenous mindset, "to proceed on the assumption that the infant church in any land must always be cared for and provided for by the mother mission is an unconscious insult to the people that we endeavor to serve, and is evidence of lack of faith in God and in the power of His gospel." Hodges notes that the apostle Paul "Stayed a limited time in one area but he left behind him a church that could govern itself; that could finance its own expenses and that extended the gospel throughout the region."

Gailyn Van Rheenen, adjunct professor of missions at Abilene Christian University, and former missionary to East

[The Indigenous Church]

Africa, examines certain challenges from the indigenous church perspective in his 1996 book *Missions* (page 202):

> Generally, indigenous perspectives appropriately apply to rural, face-to-face cultures, which do not have a high degree of specialization and do not relate extensively to the international arena. Urban situations are frequently quite international, and models of partnership are more likely to empower the church... In most urban settings developing church movements have an extremely difficult time beginning without some type of partnership with churches and agencies of other countries. Building standards are stringent, and partnering is necessary to provide the urban space necessary where rents are high...

Previous of this, Van Rheenen provides expanded terminology to express the indigenous concept, insights that are worthy of consideration (same book, pages 199-189):

> A better phrase for the indigenous concept is 'building responsible churches.' The term responsible implies many of the intended meanings of indigenous, without much of its baggage. Responsible implies that the church has grown to maturity in Christ and can now walk alongside those who founded her... The church is able to propagate itself, support itself, govern itself, and demonstrate the attributes of God in the midst of pagan society. Responsible churches are those that have grown to maturity and are fully able to reflect the attributes of God in appropriate ways within their cultural contexts"

William A. Smalley in his 1992 book *Perspectives on the World Christian Movement* defines an indigenous church as "a group of believers who live out their life, including their socialized Christian activity, in the patterns of the local society, and for whom any transformation of the society comes out of their felt needs under the guidance of the Holy Spirit and the Scriptures." This definition communicates that the church-planting missionary must be willing to allow the indigenous church to have different manifestations of Christianity (culturally relevant) rather than export their denominational or personal patterns that are rooted in the missionary's history and culture.

The missionary must understand it is not his or her place to modify the cultural framework for the indigenous church. The missionaries can be valued advisers with their knowledge of Scripture and experience in the faith. In fact, it is the missionary's responsibility to be a source for strategic alternatives for an indigenous group to select if they want and need them. However, the indigenous church leaders themselves should make ethnic decisions based on their needs, problems, values and outlooks.

The Scripture reveals that God has always dealt with people in terms of their culture. God intentionally worked His law, spirit and relationship with humanity within a particular culture. In the same manner, the missionary must read and understand the Scripture in its cultural perspective and God's dealing with humanity through different cultural situations. Additionally, the missionary must be careful not to impose and decide what course a new church plant should follow, with having little to no knowledge of the cultural background of the people. The primary mission should not be to corporatize Christianity on people nor should it be to impose their own cultural traditions.

The missionary's purpose is to preach that God, in Jesus, is reconciling the world unto Himself and the Kingdom of God is near. The goal is not to colonize, or in the case of western missions to "westernize," indigenous populations into a western worldview and culture. Therefore, a missionary must trust the Holy Spirit to mature and guide the indigenous church. An indigenous church is precisely one in which the cultural changes are taking place under the guidance of the Holy Spirit who meets the needs and fulfills the meaning of that church plant.

As an indigenous church or mission station gradually is released to its own national leadership and independent support, it grows in maturity and confidence. Like

[THE INDIGENOUS CHURCH]

compassionate and caring parents, the organization or persons that were involved in the inception of the work identify a type of maternal connection. They want to always be involved at some level because they will always care. They will be prepared to act if a need arises because they love the indigenous church, mission station, or placed leaders. But they realize that it is God's will that the indigenous work becomes strong within the context of its own leaders, in its own culture, and among its nation's people.

Even when the indigenous church has reached a level of independence whereby it should qualify for missionary disengagement there will be ways that missionaries can continue to make contributions that are both valued and desired by the national church. This is particularly true where the missionary brings special skills, ministries and perspectives to the work. Missionaries who have served for a considerable time in a country, learned the language, adapted to the culture and developed positive relationships with the national church may be effective in some situations specifically because they are not indigenous members of the host culture and are not as influenced by the internal cultural and political dynamics of the national church.

Additionally, in some instances national churches that have reached a point of self-governance and self-propagation, and are self-supporting at the local church level, may not be in a position to provide total financial support for all the ministries provided within their church plant. A degree of support may be necessary to sustain its growth for an undetermined amount of time. In essence, the traditional understanding of indigenous church principles suggests that the desired end-state of national church development is independence from the missionary body that brought it into being. It does not describe what should happen after that, except by implication, that the missionary force and support structure should continue on to the next work.

The key to the indigenous work is the concept/principle of the indigenous church: "Indigenous church planting is sowing the gospel seed in the native context of thought and things, allowing the Holy Spirit to do His work in His own time and way," writes Charles Brock in his book ***Indigenous Church Planting: A Practical Journey***. Within this concept of the indigenous church, Brock makes a very important point in saying that the church, to be indigenous, must be based and centralized in Christ and not in or on a missionary or support organization. Neither of these entities will birth an indigenous church; Christ as the base and center will allow for a spiritually healthy indigenous church. This will glorify God as it is not a transplanted Christianity, but rather an authentic understanding of the Word that plays itself out in the cultural forms of the indigenous peoples, making it unique in its forms of worshipping God in ways in which other cultures do not, or cannot realize.

This specific subject requires a good deal of study to comprehend. A must-read for every missionary church planter is the book quoted above by Melvin L. Hodges. The book consists of the combination of two books in one volume. Melvin Hodges wrote the original book "The Indigenous Church" in 1953. The book since has been revised twice. The second book "The Indigenous Church and the Missionary" was copyrighted in 1978. Some readers may consider the information and methods contained outdated. Regardless of some of the dated content, the book is a valuable and timeless resource for every cross-cultural missionary who partners with local indigenous churches or intends to plant local indigenous churches.

[21]
SUPPORT OF THE INDIGENOUS LEADERSHIP

In the early church it was customary to develop strong local leadership wherever the gospel was preached. "Ordain elders in every city," was the apostle Paul's instruction to Titus. The success of the church in that day depended on the development of local leadership. It is evident that the local leadership of the church in apostolic times was placed on the shoulders of the maturing converts just as quickly as possible. It is said that the apostle Thomas went to India, and in a few years succeeded in winning a large group to Christ, and proceeded to train local leadership. Developing native leaders in foreign church plants is a prerequisite of any effective mission strategy.

The wisdom of how to support national pastors with mission funds has been debated for many years. One recent missionary leader challenged the validity of "the arguments for self-support and the indigenous church" as early as 1977. In the 1980s, the emergence of the Two-Thirds World missionary movement raised the issue again. The churches of the West were urged to share their financial resources with the emerging missionary force. In 1992, another missionary leader strongly advocated that emerging mission dependence on western financial aid be ended by teaching the Two-Thirds World churches to give.

From the *Evangelical Missions Quarterly* in 1998, Decadal Growth Rates (DGR) of various districts were studied, to define how supported ministries compared to self-supported indigenous (native) ministries. The research focused on the years 1972-1990. The districts that received no worker support saw a clear pattern of consistent growth in the district from the opening of the first church in 1951 through to 1990. This growth was achieved totally without subsidy for its indigenous workers. The key to its growth was strong evangelistic work by its lay leaders, especially witnessing along family lines.

The measure of growth in the districts where a personal subsidy was provided resulted in a far greater financial cost with problematic results. One district grew from three churches in 1967 to 12 in 1970. The DGR for the period 1970-1980 was only 25 percent, but in the next decade it dropped to -7 percent. Thus, from the 12 churches planted without subsidy by 1970, the district grew by only two more churches in 1990 after investing $41,500 USD in national worker subsidy. The record does not indicate that subsidy had a positive impact on church growth.

When these results are considered together with the results of all the statistics from each district, one conclusion is driven forcefully home: subsidy did not have a positive impact on the growth of the national church. In fact, the growth of the church ceased when the subsidy was formally initiated. Why did the initiation of subsidy coincide with the cessation of growth? The paid ministry workers began to concentrate more on pleasing the mission's organization, which paid their salaries, and less on meeting the needs of their churches. Further, the paid workers lost the vision for evangelism and instead tended to their own needs. They increasingly reduced their attention to ministering to the needs of the immediate congregation, while neglecting to visit the neighboring villages to preach the gospel.

Additionally, when the local church congregations realized that the mission's organization was paying the salary of their native pastor, they lost their sense of ownership of their native leader. They increasingly came to see the pastor as the mission's hireling. As a result, they felt no obligation to give toward the pastor's support. When the pastor saw that the congregation was not concerned with providing for his support and well-being, he devoted himself even more to

[Support of the Indigenous Leadership]

pleasing the mission's organization that paid his salary. In time, the native pastors grew comfortable in their lifestyle, later attempting to persuade the mission's organization to increase the funding provided.

The conclusion of the study was that indigenous church congregations must assume responsibility for the support of their pastor as soon as possible, even though sometimes that choice might result in a challenging lifestyle for the native pastor. If the pastor is serving the Lord selflessly and for the sake of the Kingdom, he will walk by faith looking up instead of at other men. If the pastor is in the service for the sake of personal and lifestyle support, they will fall away after the money stream ceases.

The indigenous pastor must view himself or herself as the servant leader of the congregation. Members of the congregation must recognize their responsibility to their pastor and fulfill their obligation. This is not only common sense, but the essential framework of how church plants grow and thrive.

One of the greatest missionary movements in the church's history was initiated by the German Count Nicolaus Zinzendorf and the Moravians, who achieved a ratio of one missionary to every 12 communicant members. Eventually they had three members on the mission field for every one at home. They did this by developing creative ways of generating partial to full self-support. Using common church jargon, they became tentmakers or self-employed. They found ways to support themselves while serving with high mobility, in spite of having families.

The indigenous pastors are called by God to rise up among their people and grow self-sustaining spiritual centers of worship and learning. They are entrusted to delegate supplied funding and resources for the primary purpose of evangelism and church planting, while supporting themselves and their families through local donations and possible secular employment. This obviously varies from situation to situation, but this is the understood biblical standard.

Paul expressed this when he wrote, *"Surely you remember, brothers, our toil and hardship; we worked night and day in order not to be a burden to anyone while we preached the gospel of God to you"* (1 Thess. 2:9). Again in 2 Cor. 11:9, Paul wrote *"And when I was with you and was in need, I did not burden anyone, for the brothers who came from Macedonia supplied my need. So I refrained and will refrain from burdening you in any way."* Paul at times did receive aid, but it typically was for earnest needs like clothing and food, not provision of lifestyle. Several times Paul clarified to the Corinthians that he was not going to take their provisions: *"Now I am ready to visit you for the third time, and I will not be a burden to you, because what I want is not your possessions but you. After all, children should not have to save up for their parents, but parents for their children"* (2 Cor. 12:14). Paul felt like a father toward the church in Corinth; and he was willing, therefore, to labor among them without compensation. In Neh. 5:14-19, we read that Nehemiah refused to be a burden on his fellow countrymen, but devoted himself to the work at hand. Where are the hearts of modern Church leaders, missionaries, and native pastors regarding this detail?

In defense of indigenous pastors' support, the Scripture clarifies that it is not wrong for spiritual leadership to take some support for personal expenses, which reads, *"Let the elders who rule well be considered worthy of double honor, especially those who labor in preaching and teaching. For the Scripture says, 'You shall not muzzle an ox when it treads out the grain,' and, 'The laborer deserves his wages'"* (1 Tim. 5:17-18). Here Paul is quoting Deut. 25:4 and referring to Deut. 24:14.

We can also read Paul's defense of pastoral support in 1 Cor. 9:14, *"In the same way, the Lord has commanded that those who preach the gospel should receive their living from*

[SUPPORT OF THE INDIGENOUS LEADERSHIP]

the gospel." This counsel is that they shall live off the gospel. They should be provided what is needed to keep their minds from being overcome with survival cares that may cause them to forget their dependence on God, or on the local church body. This does not mean that the assisting mission's organization is responsible for supporting the native pastor and his family's lifestyle, but that the local church body should attempt to provide essential living support.

The weight of the writings of the Apostle does imply that if at all possible, every leader and minister of the gospel should strive to pull their own weight by continuing in an income-producing trade. In 2 Thess. 3:8, Paul writes, *"Nor did we eat anyone's food without paying for it. On the contrary, we worked night and day, laboring and toiling so that we would not be a burden to any of you."*

All blessings are from God and any donations given are to be prayerfully shared with those church plants that are proven to be discerning of God's counsel and wise in careful delegation. If a church work appears dedicated to mainly social relief services, the missions' director should cautiously ask questions, while examining the operations of the indigenous outreach being considered. In evaluation, we must be cautious to define what the motivation is behind the mission's work: social relief or evangelism?

Mission organizations must be wary of any person promoting themselves as a pastor who is seeking outside donations as full support, either locally or abroad. While a local church may choose to support their own leaders, mission donations are not meant to be used as subsidy for sustaining a personal lifestyle. Supporting a pastor or its church leaders is ultimately the responsibility of those in the local congregation first. Additional support from the outside should be delegated as the Lord guides in every situation.

Financial resources can help disseminate the gospel, and sacrificial giving is an important Christian discipline demonstrating commitment, love, and devotion to God and His purposes. But making the fulfillment of the Great Commission dependent on the church's ability to raise money is a fallacy Western Christians have uncritically, unconsciously accepted. It reflects the church's materialism and commitment to professionalized ministry. Again, this theoretically limits God's work to the measure of the church's economic prosperity.

Encouraging native ministries to depend on Western support for evangelism sends developing churches a distinct message: "In order to evangelize and send missionaries, you must have money to support those who are schooled and trained. Because your resources are limited, you must seek Western financial aid." When the Church or a para-church organization makes finances a "key" to world evangelization, the danger is that we are basing our mission strategy on cultural, materialistic values rather than biblical principles.

The history of missions is fraught with heartbreaking stories of resentments created when developing churches became dependent on outside funding. Programs are developed and workers are hired on the basis of outside subsidies and national churches come dependent on them. When missional churches have to reduce the subsidies, or when the national believers spend or hire in ways disagreeable to the supporting churches, hard feelings and misunderstandings normally result.

Any giving to mission churches or native workers must answer two questions: "Will this stimulate or discourage local giving?" and "Will it create unhealthy dependency and foreign dominance, or help the church mature and become self-sustaining?"

A person might ask, "Why don't we see churches in other countries supporting their own missionaries if that is the best policy?" A billion people, including many evangelical Christians in Asia, Africa and Latin America, cannot find employment that will provide sufficient income. They survive by growing tiny plots of rice, fishing or scavenging for food.

[SUPPORT OF THE INDIGENOUS LEADERSHIP]

Those who do have paying jobs may give generously and sacrificially; however, their wages are so meager that the total sum of their donations may only be a couple dollars a week. Unfortunately, for most of the world, poverty is the rule and wealth is the exception.

Statistics in 2013 show that the average worker in the United States earns over $58 USD per day. Compare that to a worker in Myanmar who survives on $2.73 USD per day, or a person in India who makes on average $2.38 USD per day. With so little income to be made, the support of the local church plant is impossible while they fail to provide for the basic needs of their family including food, shelter, water, and clothes.

Another question that might be asked, "Why do some missions organizations stress dedicating funding and resources for the native missionary over an occupational or short-term missionary?" A good but sometimes controversial rule is to carefully consider the value of dedicating funding to send local people so that they might work in a remote mission field, instead of supporting native people who have already given themselves to the work and would continue whether they received outside help or not. Many western missionary families require $2,500 to $4,000 USD a month to work in a foreign land where the average salary is often less than $200 USD a month. In contrast, the indigenous or native missionary is able to live on the same salary as his fellow countrymen.

Additionally, the native missionary does not require that financial resources be used to transport them thousands of miles nor do they require any special cultural or language education. All this and more add up to tremendous savings and increases the economic power of current funding and donations. For what it costs to support one North American missionary with a monthly support of $4,000 USD, it is possible to support between 20 to 25 native missionaries.

[FINDING THE BALANCE IN WORLD MISSIONS]

This is being a good steward and wise investor of God's finances and resources.

Another problem that missionaries from economically prosperous nations often face is their inability or unwillingness to live on the same level as those to whom they minister. Missionaries from better economies will often live in homes that are considered mansions to those they are trying to reach. They tend to drive trucks or cars while the natives take buses or rickshaws, and they send their children to private schools, while the natives send theirs to public school or street schools like those found under bridges or in abandoned buildings. Not only is this a costly difference, it is a social-economical gap that separates them from those they were sent to minister.

For the cross-cultural missionary, church planting is often not as difficult as the later transitional period when the occupational or short-term missionary bids farewell and the church comes under national leadership. These churches often suffer tremendously during this extraction period, lose members, and morale can become greatly discouraged. Having experienced the prestige of a trained and educated missionary as pastor, the church plant sometimes is no longer willing to accept one of its own as its leader. This is not a problem when the church is planted by an indigenous missionary and is under his leadership for the duration of their service.

In most nations that remain unreached, propaganda is a powerful issue to face as well. In such nations, social and political propaganda often promote ideologies that present western missionaries as propagandists and subversives, sent by opposing foreign governments to undermine the local government and impart new politics and religions. Such ideologies are considered to be destructive to the people and the government in power. It is unfortunate but often the goal of such propaganda is to stigmatize the foreign missionary, the message he brings, and ultimately the Christian faith.

[Support of the Indigenous Leadership]

Once again, an indigenous missionary can more readily overcome this barrier.

In India there are now approximately 1.261 billion (2014 statistics) people. An estimated 3% are Christians. In all of India today, roughly 15-20% of India's cities, towns and villages have any visible Christian witness. Though foreign missionaries are barred, God is mobilizing thousands of Indian evangelists and church planters to take the gospel to places where people have never heard of Christ before. The same is true in Burma, where the Christian population now exceeds 10 percent.

In China, 150 years of missionary work ended in 1949 when the Communists expelled 5,600 foreign missionaries. Westerners wondered if the estimated 750,000 Christians would survive the harsh rule and persecution of an atheistic government bent on exterminating those bearing the name of Christ. But today, the number of believers in China has grown to more than 150 million (2014 stats), with estimates of between 20,000-30,000 people a day coming to Christ. This, despite the fact that the China Aid Association revealed in its annual Persecution report (2014) that persecution of Christians in China continues to rise – in fact, it has increased by 38.82 percent since 2012.

In Iran there may now be as many as a million Christians, most newly converted. More people have come to Christ since the Islamic Revolution in 1979 than in all the 1300 previous years combined since Islam first came to that country. A house church movement is exploding in Iran, and the church continues to grow under indigenous leadership, in spite of intimidation and persecution.

These growth statistics repeat in almost every country where foreigners went to colonize. Foreign missionaries introduced the gospel, but then exponential growth took place in the church when national workers began to bear the responsibility of reaching those in their own country. Christianity does not thrive as long as it is perceived as a "foreign" religion. Indigenous Christians who speak the language of the people, know the culture, live life-styles consistent with their countrymen are much better suited to reach their own people.

The organization ***Advancing Native Missions*** states that:

> More than 80% of world evangelization is being done by native missionaries. Although we confidently affirm the important role that western mission organizations have played and continue to play in many regions of the world, we also know that western missions alone are not enough. As more and more countries close their doors to western mission organizations, Advancing Native Missions finds that the best way to reach these nations with the gospel is through native or indigenous missionaries: Indians reaching India, Iranians reaching Iran, etc.

In most cases, native missionaries are far more effective in reaching their own people than foreign missionaries. A native missionary can go to the places that occupational missionaries cannot. They are men and women called by God to preach the gospel and plant churches among their own people. In the eyes of the people, native missionaries do not represent a foreign country or a strange religion. They can do the job effectively because they already know the language and culture and the customs they serve, and at a fraction of the cost. A native missionary doesn't need a visa or even a passport, and they do not need to be sent: they are already there.

[22]
FIELD MISSION'S LEADERSHIP QUALIFICATIONS

Leadership qualifications consist of many traits, both personal as well as spiritual. When selecting leaders for ministry purposes, the success of any ministry is largely hinged on the enabled calling of the candidate. This is why God's Word has laid before us such challenging requirements for Christian leadership. The standards are justly high, not only for the sake of the church's vitality but also for the sake of the leader's vitality.

The chief biblical texts that develop the requirements of leaders are: cf. 1 Tim. 3:1-13, 2 Tim. 2:1-13, Titus 1:5-9, Acts 6:1-6, and Exodus 18:21-22. The qualifications spelled out in these passages can be summarized in four words: commitment, conviction, competency and character.

Commitment - Are the would-be leaders clearly committed to Jesus Christ as Savior and Lord? Is there a passion to know Him in all His fullness? While different personality types express passion differently, there must be time-tested evidence of the Holy Spirit residing in order to know and obey the crucified and risen Christ.

Conviction - Do the would-be leaders have biblically informed convictions about who God is, about the human condition, the nature of the Church, and especially the meaning of Jesus' death and resurrection? Are they learning what it means to be transformed by the renewal of the mind (Romans 12:2), to think "Christ-like" about every dimension of their lives (money, time, marriage, family, and recreation)? For this reason, Paul warns against being too quick to call recent converts to leadership; mature commitment and conviction take time to develop.

Competency – Can the would-be leaders find their way through the Scriptures? Can they help others find their way around the revelations of God (2 Tim. 2:15)? Have the would-be leaders been endued with the necessary gifts of the Holy Spirit (Eph. 4:11-12, 1 Cor. 12:12-31, Romans 12:3-8)? Do they have a working understanding of the gifts, and can they help others discern and deploy those entrusted to them? Do they have the necessary relational skills for this position? Do their relationships manifest the integrity and love of Jesus, especially in their marriage and with their children (2 Tim. 3:5)? The Kingdom of God, after all, is about righteousness; that is, a right relationship.

Character - Are the would-be leaders taking on the character of Jesus? Someone has astutely observed, "It is not a matter of perfection, but direction." Are the potential leaders moving toward greater Christ-likeness? Do they exhibit self-control, hospitality, gentleness (control of anger), a quest for holiness, temperance? Are they faithful to their spouse? Or is the flesh in control? Is there evidence revealing the love of money? Control without flexibility? Do they want a leadership role for the sake of power?

The following list enumerates fourteen key indicators of a person suitable for the work of God as a leader. While not an exhaustive list, it does provide some very important details that can be used to profile a leadership candidate for spiritual service.

1. Effective ministry leaders proclaim and inspire others to pursue the mission of the Church, such as the need to bring new believers to Christ. The skills required for leadership involve the setting of goals that utilize the abilities of the ministry team, and the ability to inspire these people to believe the goals can be achieved.
2. Ministry leaders encourage teamwork and a sense of urgency to fulfill the church's mission while ensuring that weaker team members don't undercut the leader's strategies and the church's vision. These leaders are

[Field Mission's Leadership Qualifications]

skilled in helping people grow in their ability to serve in ministries and take quality time to address a co-workers concerns and issues. Effective leaders are also able to earn the trust of the people serving under them.

3. Some leaders stand out because they often speak about the importance of quality leadership and are enthusiastic about making a difference in peoples' lives. Natural leaders lead effectively, mainly because they have a clear vision of the work that God has called them to do. Their ministries thrive under their guidance because these leaders enjoy challenges and are capable of empowering people to conquer obstacles. These leaders can passionately handle multiple ministerial duties successfully, and their experiences continually give them new skills to enhance their service.

4. Many leaders are not aware of their potential to lead ministries but develop gifts over time. Sometimes, people with potential are too modest and lack the confidence to step forward, where instead their friends recommend them for leadership positions. When something needs to be changed or improved in a ministry, undeveloped leaders respond by showing initiative and the skills to address the situation. They also are reliable and able to serve with integrity, earning the admiration of people who serve with them. New leaders must be found mature in the faith and in life, worthy of their calling in Christ Jesus. They must not be lazy or disorganized, since such people cannot be trusted as effective leaders. On the opposite extreme, effective service of a quality leader is not the result of overwork, but of overflow—the overflow of the life of intimate fellowship with Christ.

5. The Bible reveals that in the last days people will become lovers of themselves. Examine a prospective leader to see if he or she is a lover of monetary gain or possessions, since those who would press intentionally

for financial support are probably persuaded by self-interests and the love of money. Paul commands Timothy to avoid those who are lovers of money, writing a word of warning, *"Have nothing to do with such people."* (cf. 2 Tim. 3:1-9).

6. Honesty is a pillar found holding up a quality leader. Solomon wrote *"A fool's mouth is his ruin, and his lips are the snare of the soul"* (Proverbs 18:7). If a leader is not honest, their deception will soon be discovered; and the morale and motivation of the people will suffer. A leader is often tempted to alter the truth to cover up a mistake or failure. Being forthright and honest is clear evidence that he or she is taking responsibility and despite his or her faults, has integrity.

7. A good leader is a great communicator. The essential proof of this quality being resident is their ability to keep others informed. A person who does not communicate with those around him or her will not succeed as an approved leader. Paul was an avid communicator, which we can read in Col. 4:7-9, 2 Tim. 4:11 and 4:20, and Romans 16:21. He kept people engaged with the movement, aware of their function, assigned with tasks, active in prayer and earnestly motivated.

8. Positive expectation is also an important attribute of a successful leader. Any leader who focuses on the difficulties so adamantly that they cannot discern the possibilities cannot inspire vision in others. Additionally, a quality leader will not procrastinate when faced with a decision, nor vacillate after making it. James 1:8 tells us what such a person is like, *"He is a double-minded man, unstable in all he does."*

9. Regarding the quality of longsuffering, any leader who is impatient with a weakness of others will not be edifying in his or her leadership role. Paul wrote in Romans 15:1, *"We who are strong ought to bear with the failings of the weak."* Again in Romans 14:1,

[Field Mission's Leadership Qualifications]

he says "Accept him whose faith is weak, without passing judgment on disputable matters." A quality leader extends grace and forgiveness when mistakes are made. They pace those under them until the team is ready for greater challenges.

10. A pastor or leader can have a brilliant mind and possess impressive administrative skills, but without a contrite submission to God through Christ, he or she is incapable of providing God-approved spiritual leadership. Spiritual leadership is the opposite of what we would naturally think. It is about having a servant's heart that considers others first. They will be empathetic to the needs and weaknesses of others without judgment. Jesus taught us saying, *"Just as the Son of Man did not come to be served, but to serve, and to give his life as a ransom for many"* (Matt. 20:28).

11. A quality leader is selfless, as Paul demonstrated in his total consecration to the spirit of his calling, discipleship and adaptability. He lived what he wrote, *"Because the gifts and calling of God are irrevocable"* (Rom. 11:29). The apostle adapted to cultural, social and political changes and, in this way, never lost his relevant position (1 Cor. 9:19-22).

12. As a spiritual leader, a person must outpace the rest of the church in prayer and devotion to study of the Scripture. Prayer will keep the moral compass directed, spiritual vision sharp, and discernment of the Spirit's leading crystallized. E. M. Bounds states in his book ***Prayer and Praying Men*** that "Great leaders of the Bible were not leaders of brilliancy of learning, because they were exhaustless in resources, because of their magnificent culture or native endowment, but because, by the power of prayer, they could command the power of God." Daily prayer and Bible reading is not an elective, it is a requirement. When a people detect that their leader is neglecting these spiritual disciplines,

their confidence wanes and loyalty lags. Confusion about purpose replaces motivation. Lethargy replaces morale, and the enterprise will begin to die without a heart fully consumed with God.

13. When God finally calls a leader out, they should not refuse due to a sense of inadequacy. No one is innately worthy of such office in themselves. When Moses resisted, God became angry (Exodus 4:14). A few days before his death, Martin Luther stated, "I was afraid of nothing: God can make one so desperately bold." A leader must go forth in the confidence of Christ residing and guiding alone.

14. Finally, let's look at James 3:1 as the last consideration about the qualifications as a leader. The passage states that *"Not many of you should presume to be teachers, my brothers, because you know that we who teach will be judged more strictly."* This fondness for the office of teacher or leader by people who innately desire control is a vice carried into the church when they were converted, and it is this which the apostle here rebukes. If there is anything which ought to be managed with extreme prudence and caution, it is that of appointing people into the Christian ministry as leaders. There would be scarcely anything more injurious to the cause of the Church than a prevailing desire for the prominence and importance which a person has in virtue of being a pastor or leader. This caution is still necessary since there are multitudes, which God has never called, and never can call, because He has never qualified them for the work, who earnestly desire the office of leader.

[23]
How May I Get Involved?

As J. Hudson Taylor, the founder of the China Inland Mission (now OMF International) once pointed out, "The Great Commission is not an option to be considered; it is a command to be obeyed."

Whether you're a carpenter or cattle rancher, painter or plumber, bookkeeper or baker, typist or teacher or simply have a passion for missions, there's a place for everyone in God's global outreach. World-wide missions is the work of the Church. God entrusted His people with the privilege and responsibility of proclaiming the gospel of the Kingdom in word and deed to all the nations of the world.

The purpose of this book is to urge the reader's heart toward the biblical standard for evangelism and missions. As a result, you may find the Holy Spirit is guiding you to either become actively engaged with missions or to financially support the work of missions. As such, we would encourage you to seek any missions opportunities supported through your local church or any reputable para-church organization.

The majority of missions structured like Messiah Missions International, financially support native pastors and evangelists, by funding approved recipients on a monthly basis. Recipients are trained and approved leaders stationed at various locations. Support provides evangelism materials, pastor training as well as regulated funding for their growing church plants. This might include food, clothing and shelter for orphans and widows, sewing centers for the women, bicycles for evangelists, among many other needs.

Sadly, only 1% of Western donations assist the church plants in the 10/40 zone as it is called, regions 10 and 40 degrees north of the equator. They are sometimes deemed

[Finding the Balance in World Missions]

as "unreachable" or too difficult due to socioeconomic challenges. These same areas receive only 3% of the total world mission efforts. Any mission's organization needs prayer and financial assistance ongoing, where growth and potential is infinite.

Donors are often surprised to learn that $10 USD can feed an orphan child for one month in many poor countries, which is nearly the same amount for widows. Between $120 and $180 USD a month often fully supports a native missionary or indigenous pastor, including family and ministry expenses. Missionary organizations know how to stretch financial support as to meet as many needs as possible.

There are numerous ways a Christian can participate in God's plan to take the Gospel to all people groups. Listed are a few ideas for how you might get involved:

Praying
- Pray for God to send out workers into the harvest.
- Attend or create a weekly or monthly prayer meeting for missionaries.
- Sign-up to receive a missionary letters or email updates and pray for them.
- Link mission's websites and pray over adopted missions found on the internet.

Sending
- Consistently support a local or native missionary with a monthly pledge
- Write a missionary and ask if they have any special needs and then follow-through.
- When a missionary is visiting, help stock their home with supplies.
- Write an encouraging letter or email to a missionary.
- Be intentional about sending birthday and holiday cards to missionaries.

[How May I Get Involved?]

- When missionaries are visiting, set aside time to listen to their presentations.

Going
- Talk with a local mission's facilitator about how to prepare yourself for long-term missionary service.
- Become a "tentmaker," using your professional skills to gain access to another country for service.
- Go on a short-term "missions trips" only if the Lord clearly leads.
- If retired, become a missionary nanny, a dorm parent for missionary kids, or run a mission's home.

Welcoming
- Work as volunteer in a hospital, to assist patients, families and befriend those who work there as to expand diversity.
- Volunteer to help with language outreach programs for foreigners in your area.
- Learn all you can about some of the ethnic groups in the countries of interest.

Learning
- Read biographies of missionaries, especially those of historical effectiveness.
- Subscribe to a magazine like "Voice of the Martyrs" or "Mission Frontiers."
- Take any missions courses when they are offered.
- Study a foreign language that is spoken in service areas of interest.
- Obtain multiple copies of this book to share with the missions-minded.

Mobilizing
- Remain current with local and native missionaries; learn if you can physically assist at some point.

[Finding the Balance in World Missions]

- Become an advocate for a missionary you know, talking about his or her ministry with others, to help them gain new partners.
- Encourage your children or grandchildren to work locally with evangelism outreaches through inner-city services.

"'Not called!' did you say? 'Not heard the call,' I think you should say. Put your ear down to the Bible, and hear Him bid you 'go' and pull sinners out of the fire of sin. Put your ear down to the burdened, agonized heart of humanity, and listen to its pitiful wail for help. Go stand by the gates of hell, and hear the damned entreat you to go to their father's house and bid their brothers and sisters and servants and masters not to come there. Then look Christ in the face—whose mercy you have professed to obey—and tell Him whether you will join heart and soul and body and circumstances in the march to publish His mercy to the world." ~ William Booth, founder of the Salvation Army